Romance of a Little Village Girl

Pasó Por Aquí
Series on the Nuevomexicano Literary Heritage
Edited by Genaro M. Padilla,
Erlinda Gonzales-Berry, and
A. Gabriel Meléndez

Romance of a
Little Village
Girl

Romance of a Little Village Girl

By CLEO JARAMILLO

THE UNIVERSITY OF NEW MEXICO PRESS

ALBUQUERQUE

Foreword and Introduction © 2000 by
the University of New Mexico Press.

Romance of a Little Village Girl was originally published by
The Naylor Company, San Antonio, TX, in 1955.
© 1983 by Virginia M. Smith Rogers and
reprinted courtesy of the family.

First UNM Press edition

Library of Congress Cataloging-in-Publication Data

Jaramillo, Cleofas M.
   Romance of a little village girl / Cleofas Jaramillo.
     p. cm.
   Includes index.
   ISBN 0-8263-2286-7
   1. Hispanic Americans—New Mexico—Social life and customs. 2. New
Mexico—Social life and customs. 3. Folklore—New Mexico. 4. Jaramillo,
Cleofas M. 5. Hispanic American women—New Mexico—Santa Fe—
Biography. 6. Taos (N.M.)—Biography. 7. Santa Fe (N.M.)—Biography.
I. Title

F805.S75 J37 2000
978.9'56—dc21   00-03380

All illustrations reproduced courtesy of the family.

To the memory
of my beloved husband
Venceslao Jaramillo
whose beautiful life
so greatly enriched my own,
and everyone's, who
crossed his path.

Preface

It is not unnatural for one who lived a harmonious, happy young life to desire to revive those years, to people the melting ruins of a once-happy home, to live again in memory the girlhood years that were enriched with comfort and love, innocent of any wickedness, sheltered from all care and grief, and to live again among those kind, humble people, loyal to their God's religion, respectful and honest.

In this little valley of the Arroyo Hondo River, situated in the northern part of the state of New Mexico, hemmed in by high mountains and hills, sheltered from the contamination of the outside world, the inhabitants lived peacefully, preserving the customs and traditions of their ancestors. Here in this verdant little nook the authoress was born and reared until cupid found its way into it; for cupid is so smart that not even the most-hidden spots in the world ever escape his far-flung darts.

Under the apparent deadness of our New Mexico villages there runs a romantic current invisible to the stranger and understood only by their inhabitants. This quiet romance I will try to describe in the following pages of my autobiography, although I feel an appalling shortage of words, not being a writer, and writing in a language almost foreign to me. May I offer an apology for my want of continued expression in some parts of my story.

Some of the material in my first book, published under the title of *Shadows of the Past*, I have used in this work, now to be published as *Romance of a Little Village Girl*, and as a sequel to my first book.

ix

Contents

xi

Pasó Por Aquí Series Foreword

Cleofas Jaramillo, born into a pioneering family from Arroyo Hondo, New Mexico, first published *Romance of a Little Village Girl* in 1955. The book is an unusual combination of personal memoirs and of folklore collected by the author. Building on Jaramillo's earlier publications, *Romance* provides insight into her personal and professional struggles as she worked to record and recover the cultural legacy of village life in northern New Mexico. Written when she was in her seventies, *Romance* was conceived as a continuation and the culmination of her life's work. In introducing the work to her readers Jaramillo saw *Romance* "as a sequel to my first book *Shadows of the Past/Sombras del Pasado*" (Preface) but, importantly, she also thought of it as her autobiography.

Romance is a remarkable book, not merely because it expands the project, in vogue in Cleo Jaramillo's lifetime of preserving the vanishing customs of the villages, but also, by the very act of its creation, Cleo, quite unexpectedly, turns away from her "quiet romance" with the New Mexico of her girlhood, to express her struggle for personhood in mid-twentieth century America. Personal loss, the murder of her daughter, Angelica, and the politics of living in the art/tourist Mecca which Santa Fe had become in 1930s and 1940s intervene in Jaramillo's story in disturbing and unnerving ways. We are awed, inspired, and saddened by the flesh and bone concerns that inhabit Cleofas the writer, Cleofas the mother, and Cleofas the representative of her cultural group. As modern readers we are drawn to Jaramillo's

FOREWORD

life story, a story which we more clearly understand today was vexed by modern dilemmas and concerns.

First issued by the Naylor Company of San Antonio, Texas, copies of the first edition *of Romance of a Little Village Girl* have only been available in the special collections of a handful of public and university libraries in the Southwest. As the editors of the Pasó Por Aquí Series we are delighted that the long anticipated re-publication of this gem of New Mexico letters is now accessible to a wide range of readers. *Romance* presents a case where a goodly amount of solid scholarship precedes the re-issuance of the work itself. Students of Southwest literature owe a special debt to Raymond Paredes, Genaro Padilla, and Tey Diana Rebolledo for calling attention to this pioneering work in letters and for reminding us that *Romance* needs to be appreciated for the warmth of its style and understood for the complex meanings it contains. Thus, we are pleased that readers of the current edition will also hear of scholarship that has driven the rediscovery of *Romance* in the insightful introduction by Diana Rebolledo, which graces the present edition.

Pasó Por Aquí Series Editors
Erlinda Gonzales-Berry
A. Gabriel Meléndez
Genaro Padilla

Introduction

Tey Diana Rebolledo
University of New Mexico

Cleofas Martínez Jaramillo was a mother, wife, folklorist, writer, and businesswoman. Born to Marina Lucero Martínez and Julián Antonio Martínez on December 6, 1878 in Arroyo Hondo, a small northern New Mexico village, Cleofas was one of seven children, two girls and five boys.[1] Her family on both sides was influential in New Mexico. Her paternal great-grandfather, José Manuel Martínez had a Tierra Amarilla land grant of more than three hundred thousand acres, and her grandfather, Vicente Martínez, bought part of the Arroyo Hondo grant, becoming a sheep and land owner. Her maternal grandfather, Jesús María Lucero was a trader who met his wife in Chihuahua, Mexico while trading on the Chihuahua Trail. Her father was also a man who prospered because of his energy and his various business interests, which included sheep and cattle raising, farming and mercantile. Early on Don Julián learned to speak English so he could deal with traders and merchants. Her mother too was extremely hard working, not only raising her children but also helping out in the store and functioning as a médica and counselor for the entire community.

---

[1] The children included Ben, Alfonso, Tom, Reyes, Onésimo, and May.

INTRODUCTION

When she was nine years old, Cleofas attended the Loretto Convent School in Taos, New Mexico and went on to study at the Loretto Academy in Santa Fe, New Mexico. Many details of her early childhood, family life and schooling are included in her autobiography. On July 27, 1898, she married Venceslao Jaramillo, a cousin, who was already wealthy and a businessman. He was just beginning his career in politics and was an aide-de-camp to Governor M. A. Otero, although he was just twenty years old. Their married life together was lived in great comfort, but also with tragedy. Two of their children died young, and a third child, Angelina, was only four years old when Venceslao Jaramillo died. Although he had been very wealthy, because of his illness and other factors, he left his business affairs in disarray. None of the land he owned or his business interests had been in Cleofas' name, and she had to struggle to prove that she had any inheritance from him. Moreover, economic depression, business debts, high interest rates, bank failures, and unscrupulous business partners contributed to leaving the family in debt. Struggling to understand the business and to pay off the debts left her, Cleofas learned to manage what was left of her husband's estate and to become an astute businesswoman. After his death, her tragedies continued however when Angelina was murdered at the age of seventeen. Cleofas was devastated by all these events and recorded this difficult time in her autobiography. Cleofas Jaramillo was destined to live for a long time, dying in 1956 at the age of seventy-eight.

In her books, *Cuentos del hogar/Spanish Fairy Tales* (1939), *The Genuine New Mexico Tasty Recipes/Potajes sabrosos* (1939), *Shadows of the Past/Sombras del pasado* (1941), and *Romance of a Little Village Girl* (1955) Cleofas Jaramillo has left us a remarkable account of traditional customs and folklore, community life, Hispano history, and, of course, her life. She began to write, she tells us, in order to preserve Hispano traditions she felt were disappearing. These traditions were very much embedded in the oral traditions of storytelling, recipe giving, and family histories. Her mother, Marina, was a storyteller, and in *Cuentos del hogar/Spanish Fairy Tales* Jaramillo translated into English and published twenty-five of her mother's stories. In addition, her brother, Reyes M. Martínez, was active in collecting stories and tales of northern New Mexico, as he was employed as a writer by the New Mexico Federal Writers' Project. At that time, Taos, Las Vegas, and Santa Fe were undergoing a cultural renaissance because of the influx of Anglo and European writers, artists and craftspeople to the area. The Hispana writers of the period, Aurora Lucero White, Nina Otero Warren, and Fabiola Cabeza de Baca, among others, were concerned that with the intensive Americanization project that was taking place in the 1920s and 1930s Spanish language, folkways, and customs were being lost and assimilated into what had become Anglo American mainstream culture. The Nuevamexicana writers all contributed to an intensive period of collecting stories, poems, traditional plays, recipes, and other traditions and to writing them down so they could be preserved.

However, Jaramillo, in particular, felt that the "American newcomers" did not understand Hispano customs the way they should be understood. In writing about the penitentes, for example, she said, "Due credit is given to the English writers who come to New Mexico and write such interesting books from second-hand information, but I wish here to contradict some of their statements" (*Shadows,* 64). She then goes on to cite various examples of the misinformation these writers have perpetrated. She was never reluctant to criticize those she felt did not truly understand what they were writing about, but she did so in a very respectful way.[2]

Jaramillo was especially active in preserving Hispano culture, not only through her writing, but also by founding the Sociedad Folklórica. As she says, "On account of familiarity with the old customs, we had not awakened to the fact that they were worth preserving, until in recent years, and have turned our effort to revive them" (*Shadows*, 10). Moreover she tells us that after reading about how in the south some antebellum mansions were

---

[2]We must understand that in her writing Cleofas Jaramillo's perspective was that of a woman who came from a position of privilege, that of an upper class Hispano landed family. While her concerns were with the loss of Hispano rights and culture, there was no parallel concern with the Native American's loss of rights and culture. She speaks of having an Indian slave as her cook, and describes Native people with both pejorative and laudatory adjectives. And while living with them, she mentions little about their personal lives.

INTRODUCTION

opened to the public and heirlooms were displayed, she thought that if she and friends were to look in their mothers' trunks, they would find old costumes and jewelry which could be displayed at the annual Santa Fe fiesta (Weigle, *Genuine*, 20). Thus she and a few friends planned a fiesta program that evolved into La Sociedad Folklórica. Moreover, the rules that guided the Sociedad emphasized Spanish language and Spanish heritage as the members had to be of Spanish descent and meetings were held in Spanish.

Jaramillo's interest in these matters had been especially piqued when in June 1935 she saw an article in *Hollands Magazine* about Spanish and Mexican food, an article which, in her opinion, was not accurate. She thought, "Now why don't we who know our customs and dishes do something about preserving the knowledge . . . we who know the customs and styles of our region are letting them die out."[3] She also comments sarcastically that in giving the recipe for making tortillas it read, "'mix bread flour with water, add salt.' How nice and light these must be without shortening. And still these smart Americans make money with their writing and we who know the correct way sit back and listen" (*Romance,* 173).

Thus, in her cookbook, *The Genuine New Mexico Tasty Recipes: Old and Quaint Formulas for the Preparation of Seventy-five Delicious Spanish Dishes (Potajes sabrosos)* she preserves that aspect of culture embodied in native food.[4] As an interesting aside Jaramillo tells us, "In this collection of Spanish recipes, only those used in New Mexico for centuries are given, excepting one or two Old Mexico recipes" (1). Certainly this is true, but it is also clear that many of the recipes are ones that originated in "Old" Mexico and that utilize native ingredients in addition to those that came from Spain. She also exhibits a pride in the *patria chica* (New Mexico) when she tells us, in a recipe for corn tortillas, "In Old Mexico only the white corn is used, but the blue corn has a better flavor" (3).

---

[3]*The New Mexican* (Feb. 26, 1954) 26.

[4]In the 1981 and subsequent editions of the book published by Ancient City Press, there is a short biographical essay by Marta Weigle and the addition of several short pieces on New Mexican food by Reyes Martínez. The editors have also inserted chapters 8 and 14 of *Shadows of the Past.*

INTRODUCTION

As various critics have noted, this cookbook (she always referred to it as *Potajes sabrosos*) is an important element in the resistance narrative of Cleofas Jaramillo. It is in this book that she initially represents herself as the holder of knowledge, and as subject/authority. Her book is authentic because of her lived experience, her knowledge of the food and customs, and the proper preparation of that food. She implies that, if you do not have this knowledge, the food will not be properly prepared and will not taste right. I have argued elsewhere (along with Padilla and Goldman) that these personal stories intertwined with recipes form not only a sense of place rooted within cultural discourses but are also a resistance to that dominant discourse seeking to erase cultural (and culinary) history.[5]

Shadows of the Past is dedicated to the memory of her daughter Angelina "whose interest in the old Spanish folklore encouraged me to attempt writing this book." This book is a collage of family and New Mexico history, details of feast days, games and sports, descriptions of customs such as Saints' days, weddings, wakes, and other ceremonies (it also includes seven of her drawings). Jaramillo tells us, "it is my desire to preserve some of the folklore of New Mexico, and in the interest of the rising generation—so few of whom now read the Spanish language—I started some years ago to write this book in English, although because of my Spanish descent my English is rather limited, for which I crave indulgence from those who could have done better" (10). In spite of this disclaimer, *Shadows* is a richly described narrative where one not only sees the pristine and "untouched" quality of Arroyo Hondo and its environs, but also the Spanish historical presence she felt was disappearing. "Shrouding the peace of the hidden valley is the memory of landmarks and battles fought during the days when bandit bands and hostile Indian tribes terrorized the land, and hovering over the simple beauty of the villages is mystery, for who knows but that the spirits of the old witches still creep into the bodies of black cats, when the moon is full?" (12).

---

[5]See Rebolledo, "Narrative Strategies of Resistance," Rebolledo, *Women Singing,* Padilla, *My History,* Goldman, "I Yam," for more on how cookbooks, and recipes, function within cultural discourses.

INTRODUCTION

Later she tells us, "The music of the fiddle and guitar . . . still half fills the air."

Following these hints at the ghosts that are inscribed not only on the land but also upon memory, *Shadows of the Past* leads us through the secular as well as religious calendars of the towns and villages, and she intersperses the descriptions of important events and rituals with descriptions of the people who participated in them, such as the natives of Taos and the penitente brotherhood. She also includes portraits of family members, in particular striking portraits of the female members of her family. We are thus able to glimpse into the life of women of the day. For example, she describes two older aunts: Dolores, who was very religious and who adhered to strict religious customs, but who also made mistela, a fine spiced wine, and there was her grandfather's spinster sister, Aunt Cencionita who was "quite amusing. She was very stately, tall and fair, with a delicate skin, for the sun or wind never touched it. She wore her long silver braids like a crown around her shapely head, which was always covered with a silk skull cap to protect it from the air. She ground roots and herbs, rubbing them on her temples and back of her head, to cure her continuous headaches, which she said were caused by "'aire en la cabeza,' air in the head" (29). She also described her grandmother Refugio whose speciality was needlework with chaquira, bead work. Other women who appear in the book are healers and witches, as well as workers and women of the villages. Finally, in "Chapter XIX, Old Customs Vanish," she interjects a theme that will become a constant in *Romance of a Little Village Girl*, the arrival of the Americans and the loss of courtesy, hospitality, and respect that were so integral to Hispano culture. Here too, she mentions the arrival of her husband Venceslao Jaramillo, onto the New Mexican political scene. As she comments:

> Race issues between the two races began kindling. The continuance of the harmonious relations, and political tolerance became a problem. Young Ven. Jaramillo saw no other remedy but to enter politics, run for the legislature, and see that good laws were enacted to protect his people. He made the run for representative of his county and won.

INTRODUCTION

In January when the legislature convened, the Democrats lacked three members in the House of Representatives to have a majority. Having succeeded in unseating two Republican members, the hot fight turned against the Rio Arriba county Representative. They had found out that young Jaramillo was not yet twenty-one years old and was illegal to vote. His friends, members of the famous Rough Riders, Captain Maximiliano Luna and Llewellyn, Charles Spiess (the San Miguel County "Black Eagle"), and others rose to his aid. Time must be made. They brought out their most eloquent, long speeches in his favor. At last the 28th of February arrived and as the young representative walked triumphantly into the House, his friends rose from their seats with extended hands to congratulate him. (97)

Jaramillo then entered more enthusiastically into politics, won for El Rito the Spanish American School, and worked to pass laws when New Mexico was admitted into statehood that allowed the "native population" to have greater recognition and greater understanding. Still Cleofas sees that the vanishing of old customs also diminished reserve, respect, courtesy, and hospitality and that New Mexico has "become the land of haste and hurry" (97).

As stated, many of the themes and ideas commenced in *Shadows of the Past* are later picked up and elaborated in *Romance of a Little Village Girl*, as she reflects on almost seventy years of her life. Each chapter is framed in a *romance* or ballad form, blurring the lines between poetry and narrative. Thus, Jaramillo hints at traditional heroic Spanish epic poetry. Also reminiscent of that poetry is the narration of her descent from an edenic girlhood in northern New Mexico to a more ambivalent present where she feels acutely the loss of traditional New Mexican Hispano culture. Jaramillo details the Hispano perspective as the area became an American territory in 1848, and Hispano fortunes and lands were lost in the ensuing decades. In contrast Jaramillo's own father prospered over these years because of his energy, the help of Jaramillo's mother, and because "he kept up with the times." Nonetheless there were frustrating, bewildering, and ambivalent times for Nuevo Mexicanos; a fact emphasized by Jaramillo throughout her autobiography.

Part of her autobiography deals with the schooling of Hispano children. Spanish-teaching schools were established in Taos as early as 1721 and Padre José Antonio Martínez had his own college in 1826. By the time Jaramillo herself attended the convent school in Taos when she was nine, Spanish—and Hispanos—was scorned. "We were not allowed to speak any Spanish and the first English words were, 'Put some wood in the stove.'" The Taos school had only six boarders and fifty day students and the nuns had difficulty keeping the school open. After five years Jaramillo transferred to Loretto Academy in Santa Fe, where in her class there was just one other "Spanish" girl. Here, after she asked, she was allowed to formally study Spanish.

Romance of a Little Village Girl records Jaramillo's life in precise detail and, as in *Shadows of the Past*, she records the Spanish customs and rituals that governed it. It is an autobiography that contains family and community history as well as her personal narrative. Her presentation of self is a study in contrasts: she sees herself as timid and reserved while at the same time she appears as a strong woman, particularly during the hard and stressful times of her life, as when Angelina is murdered. Yet she emphasizes that she was always reserved in her manner. So too in her narrative, while she gives broad sketches with many details of her life, she nevertheless elides other important details. It is as if, always a lady, there are many things she should not reveal. She, politely, is constantly wearing her white gloves. For example, she speaks of her husband's illness but we never discover what it was. She hints at trouble with her husband's family but does not discuss those relationships further. When she finally talks about her daughter's death, we only know what she herself reveals about it to set the record straight. In remembering her daughter, Jaramillo is often critical of herself—in retrospect thinking she was too rigid in her daughter's upbringing. Moreover, her narrative is rooted in memory—the contrast between the Hispano past which is remembered as full of meaning, value and spirituality, and the present, seen as tawdry, tumultuous, chaotic, and often without meaning.

At times the discourse in *Romance* achieves a critical perspective and an underlying cultural critique. Jaramillo details the disjuncture between Anglo and Hispano culture as exemplified by the death of her first child. She had gone to a hospital in Denver in order to have good health care and yet her baby dies.

INTRODUCTION

> On the second day, when the nurse brought in the baby from his bath, I felt his little hands and they were ice cold. "The baby is so cold," I said to her. "Just on the outside," she answered, putting the baby back in his basket up on the table by the window. I almost cried. I wanted to keep him by me to keep him warm. By next day his kidneys had stopped functioning. The baby specialist circumcised the baby as a cure. He cut a blood vessel and the baby bled to death. (108)

This telling scene is contrasted in the next chapter with a discussion of what the médica, or curandera, tells her. "Hearing what had happened to our baby, the médica said: That trouble comes from catching cold. We roast an onion, split it open, and while it is still warm, place it over the baby's bladder. Muy pronto (very soon) the functioning is release" (109). The meaning is clear, if Jaramillo had given birth to her baby within her culture preserve and context, the baby would have lived.

She also criticizes the attitude of people who did not understand the value of Spanish traditions and heritage. When the old church at Abiquiu was torn down she comments, "This shows how little the new French priests appreciated the great faith (of) our ancestors who labored to build these great shrines to the honor of God" (61).

Romance is also a text where the landscape underlies the narrative content. At the beginning of the narration, Jaramillo's home is a paradise with crystal-clear springs and bountiful and verdant meadows. By the end of the narrative, this scene has completely changed. When she returns to the village the old buildings have been replaced by new and she feels only sadness and loss with "nothing alive but memories of our once lively, happy home, now in melting ruins . . . with a sigh I turned away from this sad sight" (187). The same displacement perspective that underlies the story is also clear in Jaramillo's recollection of taking Anglo writer Ruth Laughlin Barker to Arroyo Seco because Barker wanted to see old Nuevo Mexicano houses to describe in her new book. Jaramillo tries to find house after house, but they have all disappeared. "We rode on to Arroyo Seco to see the fine Gonzales home. We were standing right before it but I did not recognize it. 'Where is Juanita Gonzales's home?' I asked a man in the yard. 'This is the house,' he answered. The whitewashed porch with the blue railing post was gone and the whole house was in ruin" (119).

There are other examples where her narrative is displaced into landscape. When her first child dies, it is in the planting of her garden that she finds strength and renewal; "to bury a dry seed in the ground and see it burst through the earth as a green sprout, watch it grow, spread its branches and be covered with exquisite flowers, is a magic wand" (109). Time and time again we see how the land and the landscape is able to regenerate her. As a foreshadowing of the deaths of both her mother and Angelina, she focuses on some white geraniums she had brought into her Santa Fe house; "There is a superstition among Spanish people that when a white flower blooms in the house someone in the family will die." And when she first goes out after Angelina's death she is greeted by "a blanket of glittering snow" and "a spotless blue heaven blinded us with its brilliancy." In the last chapter it is in her house, with its three-foot-thick adobe walls (and which she calls "Rhythm in adobe") where she centers her writing self, for it has become not only a symbol of the past, but also that space imbued in memory and creation.

As has been seen, the continuance of her cultural tradition and context was of utmost importance to Jaramillo. As stated she was surely influenced by the artists and writers (such as Barker) in Santa Fe, and, even though she wrote *Romance* in English, the language issues concerned her. The loss of her native Spanish only served to emphasize what she saw as a greater disappearance of tradition and culture and she felt "alien" writing in English. In *Romance* she laments her "appalling shortage of words, not being a writer and writing in a language almost foreign to me," and she offered an apology for her "want of continued expression in some part of her story." While this apology also forms part of the oral tradition before beginning a blessing or a song as the speaker/ singer asks pardon for not being able to do it well, it is also clearly an important thread in Jaramillo's story.

In addition, Jaramillo had the feeling that she and the Hispanos were being co-opted and that people outside the culture were trying to steal her writing just as they were trying to appropriate

INTRODUCTION

the culture. Although such fears might seem paranoic, they were not groundless. In a sense Mary Austin, Mabel Dodge Luhan, and others who helped create the mystique of New Mexican culture during the period were, in effect, appropriating the culture they found so fascinating. As Genaro Padilla asserts, the "Artists were more sympathetic than usual, not marking native people negatively . . . but nevertheless essentializing them, setting them into the sediment of the earth instead of relating to them as social beings, mystifying and mythifying their cultural practices. . . . ("Imprisoned," 47.)

This appropriating discourse also functioned as a silencer for the authentic voices that existed within that culture. This is clearly seen in Jaramillo's recollections of seeking a publisher for her work. "I tried sending my manuscript to some of our Western universities. After holding it for several months they would return it, saying that they did not have the funds with which to publish it. One professor said he was writing a book. Would I permit him to use two or three of my stories in his book? I then understood. All they wanted was to read my manuscript and get ideas from it, so I decided to have it published by a small private press here in my city" (168). It was, at the same time, these same erasing narratives that forced her, and others, finally to write. While reading a book by Fosster she commented, "He should have studied the customs of our country before attempting to write and not become confused about the Spanish, Mexican and Indian" (187).

Thus, there is an explicit critique of Anglo inroads into culture. As Padilla states, it is her understanding of a culture of "lies" being told and what was at stake. At times the silence of the narrative, the gap in which the unspoken lies palpable, signals much more than what she says. For example, she signals her criticism of those she saw trying to take advantage of her either by stealing her work (as in her book), or stealing her land (as her family's land had been stolen). At one point, when talking about the lawyer Thomas Catron she states, "sometime before he had, in some way, acquired ownership of the Tierra Amarilla Grant" (54). She goes on to explain that the grant had been deeded to her great-grandfather and his sons with the proviso that no heir could sell, yet Catron managed to buy all the land and sell it.[6] She then tells us that, as a student at Loretto Academy, she and her friends would walk by Catron's home which was a mansion. Thus she understates the significance of the loss of land, while at the same time pointing it out, a technique that is utilized many times in the text.

As Genaro Padilla explains, the alienated "I" in voicing its "uncertainty, hesitance, nostalgic sentiment often belies(s) a certain unclarified resentment and opposition." He argues that our antepasados (including Jaramillo) understood what was at stake in the act of self-representation: it was a reappropriation of one's own subjectivity—against what was considered to be historical distortions. In fact he sees two almost distinct narrative voices in *Romance,* one which narrates the difficult everyday sequences of her life, "an increasingly anguished personal history," the other a sentimental, idyllic "narrative of ethnohistorical events" *(My History,* 199).

For Padilla too, it is her "almost single-handed organization of La Sociedad Folklórica" that must be regarded as a gesture of resistance to Anglo domination. I have argued elsewhere that all of her books are a conscious set of strategies of resistance to that domination ("Narrative Strategies"). She continuously and consciously reminds us about this Anglo domination while stating that they may try to dominate as much as they want, but they do not really understand the true meaning of Hispano culture. Padilla sees embryonic resistance in the site of negotiation starting with the recipes and ending with the "quiet" romance. Given the cultural and historic times in which she was raised and lived, I see much more of a full blown, although subtle, one.

Overall Cleofas Jaramillo's story is one of faith, struggle, and survival. At the end the emphasis lies on her involvement in the preservation of culture and tradition, and in her self-authorization to do so. She gained the courage to write and to survive

---

[6]However, her brother Reyes Martínez tells us that her father, as one of the heirs, was paid $2,000 for the land. This is the money he used to start his successful business and to buy land and livestock in Arroyo Hondo. (Reyes Martínez, "The Martínez Family," 3.)

INTRODUCTION

from her husband, from her daughter, and from herself. As she tells us, when Ven was dying, "As the cord of his life broke, I felt something rush into my hand. Was this undescribable thing something of my husband's spirit that passed into me, through my hand? Was this what gave me the courage and strength needed? Something appeared to be holding me up and leading me. It seemed to say, 'Your baby needs you and there is work for you. Brace up'" (128). Aligning herself with her family, history, and community she is, at last, able to transcend the sorrows and difficulties of her life and to become whole. And as Padilla has also pointed out, it is finally in her writing, inscribing that complex and, at times, conflicted place of subjectivity, that her autobiography becomes not just a personal history, but also a political one.

Sources:

Goodman, Anne. "'I Yam What I Yam': Cooking, Culture and Colonialism." In *De/Colonizing the Subject: The Politics of Gender in Women's Autobiography*. Sidonie Smith and Julia Watson, eds. Minneapolis: University of Minnesota Press, 1992, 169–95.

Jaramillo, Cleofas, *Cuentos del hogar/Spanish Fairy Stories*. The Citizen Press, 1939.

————. *The Genuine New Mexico Tasty Recipes (Potajes sabrosos)*. Seton Village Press, 1939, 1942. Reprinted Santa Fe: Ancient City Press, 1981.

————. *Romance of a Little Village Girl*. San Antonio, Tex.: The Naylor Company, 1955.

————. *Shadows of the Past*. Seton Village Press, 1941. Reprinted Santa Fe: Ancient City Press, 1972.

Martínez, Reyes M. "The Martinez Family of Arroyo Hondo." WPA, 234. December 11, 1936. New Mexico State Archives.

Padilla, Genaro M. "Imprisoned Narrative? Or Lies, Secrets, and Silence in New Mexico Women's Autobiography." In *Criticism in the Borderland*, Hector Calderón and Ramón Saldívar eds. Durham, N.C.: Duke University Press, 1991, 43–60.

Padilla, Genaro M. *My History, Not Yours. The Formation of Mexican American Autobiography*. Madison: The University of Wisconsin Press, 1993.

Rebolledo, Tey Diana. "Cleofas Martínez Jaramillo." *Notable Hispanic American Women*. Diane Telgen and Jim Kamp, eds. Detroit: Gale Research, 1993, 219–20.

Rebolledo, Tey Diana, "Las Escritoras, Romances and Realities." In *Pasó por aquí*. Erlinda Gonzales-Berry, ed. Albuquerque: The University of New Mexico Press., 1989, 199–214.

————. "Tradition and Mythology: Signatures of Landscape in Chicana Litereature." *The Desert is No Lady; Southwestern Landscapes in Women's Writing and Art*. Vera Norwood and Janice Monk, eds. New Haven: Yale University Press, 1987, 96-124.

————. *Women Singing in the Snow: A Cultural Analysis of Chicana Literature*. Tucson: The University of Arizona Press, 1995.

Weigle, Marta. "About Cleofas Martínez de Jaramillo." *The Genuine New Mexico Tasty Recipes*, Santa Fe: Ancient City Press, 1981, 19–20.

The author as a
young lady in 1901,
posed in her New York
hat with her sister

Col. Venceslau Jaramillo
as militia aide to Territorial
Governor Miguel A. Otero.
Albuquerque, New
Mexico 1897

Col. and Mrs. Venceslao
Jaramillo wedding
portrait while on their
honeymoon trip, 1898

Cleofas Jaramillo
with mantilla
c. 1900–1910

Cleofas Jaramillo
c. 1898–1900

Folklórica's Ten Year Jubilee. La Fonda Hotel, Santa Fe, June 15, 1945.

Marina de Martínez Lucero
(the author's mother)

The author's
daughter
Angelina
(Angie) probably
17–18 years old

CHAPTER I

The New Spanish Province

"The first white speck on the
Western sea was made by a Spanish
sail,
And the first lonely grave on the
plains,
Was dug by a Spanish trail.

"They left their loved abodes
To tempt new seas, and stretched
their sails,
Full-blown before the driving gale —
Theirs to be submissive to fate
Self-sentenced, yet elate,
Fearless o'er trackless waste to fly
To lands unsettled to habitate."

Romance and adventure have always ridden hand in hand with the Spanish race.

When wise Columbus conceived the idea that there was land across the Western sea and, with the aid of Queen Isabel of Spain, outfitted an expedition, and in wind-tossed vessels dared the perils of an unknown sea, he was not only seeking discoveries but also adventure and romance.

Intrepid Cortez, Coronado and Oñate and brave De Vargas, and many other explorers and colonizers followed after him, with the same urge. They brought with them colonists and missionary priests. Toiling and suffering untold hardships, they penetrated through mountain passes, across vast prairies, conquering savage Indian tribes and establishing settlements in wildernesses. Developing farms, they raised scant crops for their maintenance. The missionaries built churches appalling in their construction. They helped carry the faith and culture of old Spain into these remote worlds. Hardships only meant exciting adventure; they did not discourage the Spaniards' desire to discover and conquer.

By 1680 there was so much of Old Spain here in New Spain that the new province had begun to flourish. Just then the Indians rebelled against Spanish rule, secretly rose in revolt, and massacred the soldiers and missionaries. The soil of New Spain was reddened by the blood of the martyrs. In the Santa Fe region, only a few of the Spaniards, who fled to El Paso, escaped. For twelve years, the Indians were left in sole possesion of the land.

With stern determination, the Spaniards led by brave Gen. De Vargas returned. With but a handful of soldiers he recaptured the capital, Santa Fe, and became governor of the vast province. He again started to replant the seed of Spanish culture and faith.

Following the final reconquest of the hostile Indian tribes, the kings of Spain did everything to encourage settlement of the new country. Grants of land were made to those interested in crossing the ocean. The vastness of the country appealed to those who came. They wrote letters to their kinsmen telling them of the richness of farms and grazing lands. Many others came, with their families and retinues to populate the grants. Among the lucky men who received a large grant in the early 19th Century was Capt. Sebastian Martin. With his large family and forty other families he established a settlement on the grant near the Rio Grande above the Indian pueblo, "Pajaro Azul."

This was a wilderness inhabited only by Indians. To protect themselves from the savages, the captain had a wall

2

THE NEW SPANISH PROVINCE

built around the village and the church which he had built for the people.

Later, informed that the governor, Capt. Tomas Velez Cachupin, to relieve the unemployment of the increased population in his village, favored opening a new settlement at Rio de Las Trampas, Capt. Martin proved his generosity by donating 1,640 *varas* of land along the river to the families named to settle it. In the 19th Century the Martins dropped the "Serrano" and adding a "Z" to "Martin," gave it a plural ending, "Martinez."

Earlier, some of my ancestors, the Luceros, descendants of Pedro de Godoy, settled the little valley of Ojo Caliente, which had already been discovered by Sosa and by Cabeza de Baca.

In time the sons of the Luceros grew up. Cupid came whispering into their ears about the wealthy Sebastian's daughters. Julian Lucero tried his luck first. Taking flight on cupid's wings, he found himself inside the walled village where romance awaited him. Not long after, Julian and Barbara Martin were pledging troth before the altar in the little church. Then came Santiago Lucero, who met with the same good luck and married one of Sebastian's granddaughters. Don Sebastian gave the two girls land from his grant, and the Luceros built their homes on these lands, starting the village of Los Luceros.

Their sons grew up with the spirit of adventure inherited from their ancestors. Antonio Lucero de Godoy, one of Santiago's sons, figured prominently in the army of Gen. De Vargas during the reconquest of New Mexico. Andres, a grandson, outfitted an army at his own expense and won the battle at El Vado. Andre's son defeated the Comanches in a battle at San Miguel. These Luceros were brave men who helped their government establish peace and prosperity in spite of the obstacles that confronted them.

In 1835, a Martin descendant, Don Manuel Martinez, my great-grandfather, sent in a petition to the Excelentisima Deputacion at Mexico City to present his petition to the government to grant him, his eight sons and neighbors some

3

land up the Chama River, saying that being in possession of the same lands of his ancestors who came with the Oñate expedition in 1598 and established this settlement north of the Indian pueblo at Abiquiu, he found he could not make any progress on account of the Indian raids on his stock and the spent soil. The Government heard his petition and gave the Martinez family the Tierra Amarilla grant of over three hundred thousand acres, the richest grant in water, timber and grazing land in the northern part of New Mexico.

Up the Chama River Don Manuel moved his family, retinue and stock, and founded a settlement near the present town of Park View. One of his four daughters had married into the Lucero family. Another had married Gen. Jose Maria Chavez. The Spanish king, Alfonso, had rewarded him and his brother for their distinguished service by adding two more gold crosses to their coat of arms.

Don Manuel's sons were restless, energetic men. Not even the rich big grant could hold them; they must seek more adventure. Three of the sons left for Taos County, two settled at Ranchitos, and my grandfather, Vicente, bought lands at Arroyo Hondo. There he built a seventeen-room house, where afterwards my parents lived and raised their family of five boys and two girls.

What was that brave spirit of adventure that lured our ancestors to leave the comforts of their European abodes to come into this wilderness among savages? Was it the urge of discovery, of a change of scene? This was the case of young Cristobal Larrañaga, a general in the army of King Carlos III. Letters received from kinsmen telling about the richness of the lands and beauty of the Taos valley in the northern part of the new province induced him to embark for the new world about 1780, bringing with him his wife, his two children, Miguel and Pablita, and his brother, Ramon, and family. They met with stormy seas; his wife died in mid-Atlantic and was buried at sea. Bereft but not undaunted, the travelers after a long, hazardous journey from the port where their vessel put in, reached Taos.

Cristobal soon found an outlet to his unbounded energy

4

in establishing a new home for his family and developing his land in his newly-found country. He soon was a leader in his community, interested in the education and culture of the young, and always ready to help others in all their needs.

In a few years, Pablita, his daughter, grew up into a young lady and marriel Pablo Lucero, a son of the founder of La Placita de Los Luceros, on the Rio del Pueblo, in Taos. In those early days the daughters of the rich were educated at home. Pablo hired a tutor to teach their daughter, Luz, and her mother, Pablita, taught her poetry and music from books they had brought across the sea. Luz grew up beautiful. She had many suitors and married young to Santiago Martinez. They had a large family of eight children. All of these children were given the best education that could be acquired in those days. They were all talented, showed great interest in literature and music, and had great appreciation for art, contributing thus to the preservation of culture of the valley. Miguel wrote poetry and historical data of important events that occurred in Taos. Tiofilo and Pablo enlisted in the U. S. Army during the Civil War. Inocencio was a born scholar. When he grew up he was Taos County secretary for many years. Most of the early records are in his handwriting. He also had musical talent. When he was attending Padre Martinez' school, the priest noticing this talent, bought him a violin and encouraged him to take up the study. Later he became a famous musician, composed his own music and played in concerts and dances in different towns. I remember the excitement when he came to Arroyo Hondo to play at big wedding dances. My father called him cousin. His son-in-law, Andres Bernal, was the first public school teacher at Taos.

There was a great variety of names among my fathers' relatives. I don't know how he ever kept track of them, but he seemed to know them all — and all these relatives stopped at our house.

CHAPTER II

Government Changes Take Place

Years had passed. Mexico had won its independence from Spain under the leadership of Gen. Iturbides. The Mexican government concerned itself but little about this northern province, except in collecting heavy taxes from its inhabitants.

By now the East had found the West, and the United States government, learning of its rich resources, cast a covetous eye westward. In 1846 it sent Gen. Kearney with an army to capture the capital, Santa Fe. This was easily accomplished. Gov. Armijo with his soldiers had already abandoned the capital to its fate and left for El Paso. The people had no means to resist the intruders. Mayor Vigil in terms of honorable surrender gave up the capital. Cannons boomed announcing the conquest of New Mexico by Gen. Kearney.

The royal yellow and red flag of Spain over the *Palacio Real*, seat of Spanish rule and headquarters of this vast province, replaced first by the red, green and white of Mexico, now gave way to the stars and stripes of the United States. The last phase of Spanish rule passed.

After existing, surrounded by struggle of life and death, quelling the savage Indians, for almost three centuries under Spanish rule, with one stroke the new colony was brought under the rule of a foreign government, under a new, un-

6

GOVERNMENT CHANGES TAKE PLACE

known constitution, which helplessly the Spanish population must accept. Soberly they watched the influx of new immigration. In the wagon trains that crossed the plains to New Mexico, under armed government escorts, came such history-making men as Charles Bent, Christobal Carson, Lucian Maxwell and others. These men settled in Taos and married into prominent Spanish families. Kit Carson, the famous scout, married the beautiful Señorita Josefa Jaramillo. Bent married her sister, Maria Jaramillo, and opened a store and established trade between the states and Mexico. A new era of prosperity started. Over the dusty surfaces of the Santa Fe and Chihuahua Trails now moved the commerce of two nations. Many lives it cost to bring the new prosperity.

Charles Bent, being of a strong, friendly personality, was elected first governor of the territory under American occupation. He filled the executive chair until assassinated in Taos during the rebellion in 1847.

Adventurers, trappers, wise-eyed gamblers and towering gold seekers soon found their way here. They trekked in and discovered even the little hidden valley of the Arroyo Hondo, situated in the northern part of Taos County. This verdant little basin lies low between two high ridges of hills, closed up on the east and west by the river canyons. It is isolated from the rest of the world. Through the center of the basin splashes the noisy, rocky river. Its crystaline waters create green-carpeted meadows and fields. On the west the river surges through the stupendous gate of the Rio Grande and mingles its crystal waters with the musky green ones of the Rio Grande. Three picturesque villages add charm to this small section of the beautiful Taos Valley.

Following Kipling's advice — "There is gold in the mountains, go find it" — a hoary old mining prospector with his pack mule and wolf dog trotting beside him, descended the steep hill of the Cañoncito de San Antonio and camped by the bed of the Arroyo Hondo River. While washing his supper dishes in the river water, something shining caught his eyes. Gold! Yes, gold! This potent word soon spread

7

through the valley; even women deserted their homes and took to the river bed. Pan after pan of sand they washed. Gathering the precious gold ore, they filled thimbles with the glittering grains and took them to goldsmiths at Taos to have them made into lace-like filigree *"coquetas" or "arracadas,"* for dainty pink ears of their little girls.

The placer mining soon gave out, and the prospectors moved up the river. Beyond the San Antonio villages they found the entrance into the higher canyon of the river. A few miles further in, where the Sangre de Cristo Range climbs high into towering peaks, they discovered gold and copper. "Gold Hill" they named it. A boom struck the canyon. Two log cabins, those of Twining and Amizett, sprang up amidst majestic pine and aspen groves. Miners lured by the glamour of gold ore filled the canyon. William-Fraser's Company was formed and put up a mill, bringing the ore down the mountain in buckets by cables. Riot and speed increased as years went by, drowning the quiet that had surrounded the villages before.

By then the placer mining in the lower canyon had turned into the *"viejo Toles vinateria"* — old Turley's distillery. "Taos brightnir" began flowing into barrels. Turley fattened hogs with the sour mash and sold the pork meat and lard to the miners. His peons got drunk with the *"tisguin."* Saloons and gambling places opened. The natives found that this Anglo liquor gave more zest to tired bodies, and they set aside the soft grape wine of the Rio Abajo. Wives became worried. What was in this new drink that made their husbands so quarrelsome? Dances, games and races now ended in fist fights. The Spanish Dons could not prevent their leisurely sons from patronizing these gambling places and squandering fortunes. Eventually it dawned on the parents that times had changed and the new generation was changing with them. The only remedy they could see was to send their sons to Eastern schools, where they could learn the English language, and deal with this energetic race. Some of these boys came back from Georgetown and other schools speaking good English but still playing the part of the fine gentlemen they had been brought up to be. They would not take to work. The fortunes of the Dons soon passed out into the hands of the strangers, for minimum sums. Adobe mansions began to crumble into ruins, their owners having lost their means to keep them up. Hand-hammered silver and fine jewelry were the next thing they had to part with. Servants were discharged and Doñas now became their own maids.

Crushed at first with this hard change, but with their spirits still strong, with inherent courage and religious resignation, they bore their trials. In an effort to keep satisfied and cheerful, feast days, weddings, and other celebrations were kept up, with feasting, music and dancing.

Our families now remained more secluded in our enclosed *placitas* courtyards. Expecially after one evening, on Santiago's feast day, when a drunken *gallero* mistook our home for someone else's and spurred his horse through the back *saguan* door into our courtyard and caught his head on a wire line. Hearing his swearing, Erineo, our house servant, came out and with difficulty, disentangled the man and led his horse out on the road, but not until the man had caused great excitement among us children. After this event, mother had Erineo lock the *saguan* doors earlier. Then we were free to come out and play our favorite games in the *placita*.

9

CHAPTER III

Pleasant Outings

The country had adjusted itself to the new changes, and prosperity had helped my father's business. His chief industries were sheep raising, farming and mercantile. But being so energetic, he touched on almost every kind of work.

Occasionally on Sundays father and mother sought relaxation from their heavy responsibilities and took the family out on the long rides and picnics. It was sheer delight to roll along in our horse-drawn buggy, gradually winding up fragrant, timbered hills, past remote villages silently drowsing on green carpet valleys. Or we rode across wide plains to the foot of high mountains and through Taos' scenic canyons.

I can still see myself, like a wild bird set free of a cage, running from one berry bush to another, filling my little play bucket, my heart beating with delight at the sight of beautiful mariposa lilies, blue bells, yellow daisies, feathery ferns — plucking some to trim the pretty sunbonnets mother made for me.

My brothers found these places a fisherman's and hunter's paradise. They caught long strings of speckled mountain trout in the streams. In lakes they found wild ducks, and on prairies they hunted wild rabbits, hen, quail and other game.

Even on these outing days, pleasure was combined with

usefulness. Lupe, our cook, and Nieves, the nurse, filled flour sacks with wild hop blossoms, to be dried and kept for winter use. These were steeped in hot water and the water used to make the bread yeast. They picked berries and chock cherries for preserves.

Refreshed by the invigorating pine-fragrant air, my parents returned with renewed energy to take up their numerous tasks. Both were equally energetic. They had time for everything — work, hospitality, religion and even politics. While my father lived at Arroyo Hondo, his political party never lost their election in that precinct. He ran his combined dry goods and grocery store without help. He directed the work on his farms, and his lands produced all kinds of grain, vegetables, fruit. He raised beef, sheep, pork and race horses. These were his chief industries, but there was no limit to his ambitions. He branched out into many others. He read his Bible and kept in it a record of the births and deaths of members of his family.

In the backyard was the blacksmith shed, where wagons and farm implements were repaired and horses shod. In the carpenter shop was done all kinds of woodwork. My father, always keeping up with the times, took a notion to tear down the old-style porches and replace them with new white ones. The old ones had the best woodwork — thick round posts, carved lintels and scroll-cut corbels supported the round beams and the time-stained ceilings. The whole house was built in the best New Mexico architectural style of any old-style house I have ever seen. My grandfather, Vicente, had his wealthy father, Don Jose Manuel, to help him.

At nine years old, when I attended my Uncle Tobias' school, my father had Jose Manuel, the carpenter, make a little desk for me exactly like my teachers', but painted the brightest red. He also ordered him to make a pew to be put in the old church, where there were no seats, for our family.

My mother did her share of the work, raising her large family of five boys and two girls. She kept three, and sometimes more, servants busy. If my father was out busy with the peons and someone came who wanted something at the store, mother dropped her work and went and waited on the customer. Our store supplied the simple needs of the people, from dry goods and groceries to patent medicines, which mother would tell the people how to use.

Change of work was their relaxation. My father found it in cool eveinngs directing Erineo in planting the vegetable garden, and mother in bringing the children out to pick currants and gooseberries for jellies, and for the pies we were so fond of. Lupe and Nieves found relaxation in going out to the green bean or green pea beds to pick large dishpans full. Then fat Lupe would sit on the kitchen porch, with her legs stretched out to rest her tired feet, and called us children to help her shell the peas.

The compensation for an everyday full day's work was not material, but rather the kind that is felt in the soul. The satisfaction of having accomplished something, of doing even the small things right. For the servants it was satisfaction of doing their duty well.

Harvest time was the busiest and the happiest. I loved the loud "gid-up" and the loud cracking of the long whip that kept the herd of wild horses running around the golden wheat and oat stacks until the stacks were trampled to the ground. Then came the rumble of heavy wagons loaded with the riches of the fields to fill granaries to the ceiling. On moonlit, Indian summer evenings, it was fun to sit around the corn pile, helping to husk the corn, while listening to the witty jokes and stories of our houseservants or of neighbors who came to help. Then, later, sitting in front of a warm fireplace to watch the shelling. The corn was roasted in the large adobe oven, or boiled in lime until it pealed, then spread to dry in the sun and sent down to our log, water-run mill, to be ground into meal, and brought back to the house to be sifted and sacked.

The beeves and porks were then butchered. Hundred-pound cans were filled with the rendered pork lard. From the residue, large kettles of hard soap were made. The fruit from the big orchard that father planted across the river was picked and brought in.

PLEASANT OUTINGS

The abundance of those times now are past, even out in the country. The new generation doesn't like farming. Our home was so abundantly supplied, it was always ready to receive unexpected, uninvited guests, some just passing through. Even traveling men who came to take papa's orders for the store found some excuse for stopping overnight. With that old hospitality, they were always cheerfully received. After the harvesting was over came the general housecleaning. Mattresses, blankets and carpets were washed with amole root soap suds in a long trough by the river. The walls were whitewashed inside and on the porches. Floors were smoothly plastered.

The *capilla* was treated in the same way. Religious Grandpa Vicente had built this family private chapel by the house. After the whitewash on the walls dried, the many holy pictures were hung back in their places. There were two especially beautiful ones, one of the Holy Family painted by Manuel Maceda in 1852 at Guadalajara, Mexico, and the other, also an original, of the Madonna. In it, the Virgin's face was so beautiful that I used to climb up on the altar to get a closer view at it. I loved this picture, which looked to me like a very good copy of Raphael's "Madonna."

In those days the stores did not carry childrens' ready made clothes. All items of clothing, from undervests to ruffled, sailor-collared blouses for my four younger brothers, and my laced and ruffled dresses, were made at home. Mother made her babies' layettes by hand from the sheerest nainsook. She never dressed her boys in overalls, and short pants were hard on long-stocking knees; her mending basket was never empty.

She cured all our ills, from measles to tonsilitis, without aid of a doctor. Herbs have medicinal virtue, and our mountains and fields are full of them. That was all she needed. My father brought vaccine from the doctor in Taos and vaccinated all the family and some of the village children. It took so well that we never had to have it done again.

With all this work to attend to, poor mother had time to visit even her sisters only once in several months. Then it al-

13

ways had to be on a Sunday, though they lived near. Too busy to develop boredom, she was always cheerful and happy. There seems to be no better tonic for happiness than work. Everyone was happy in those days. The peace that laid over the land imparted to its inhabitants satisfaction and contentment. How could people be otherwise, living according to God's laws and close to the good earth and the natural beauties of nature? Beauties were there that not even the most gifted artist can copy. The real tints of a glowing sunset, when the sky seems on fire or is suffused in delicate rose and gold. Those autumn colors on trees and shrubs covering mountains, and on wooded rivers. The crystal-like sheen on the river water, and the murmur as it splashes on its way. What sweeter music is there to soothe tired minds and nerves of hard-working people?

These good people made use of God's gifts and relaxed in their beauties, while living from the good earth's natural resources.

Children fed with simple food raised on their lands, and housed in neat little whitewashed houses with large sunny yards, were healthy and happy, too. But they were quiet and respectful, not spoiled by too much liberty and by the bold example they learn now from television and movies. Juvenile delinquency? — No one knew what it meant. People's lives radiated between church and home. Mothers stayed home taking care of their children, satisfied to live on their husbands' earnings. They were not buying new clothes all the time nor visiting beauty shops. No one was ever late for church, although some of them lived two and three miles distant and rode in slow wagons or even walked. How nice it would be if people now would live thus!

My parents were scrupulously strict in the performance of their duties, but always gentle and patient. I never heard them raise their voice to correct anyone. They lived with spiritual dignity and respect. Although never demonstrative in their affection toward their family, there was no need of display. We felt their love in everything they did for us. Mother was so refined. Once on the way to Church she noticed my gloveless hands, saying: "Bare hands?" This was enough for me not to forget my gloves again.

She often quoted from her book of *Urbanidad y Buenas Maneras.* Her favorite proverb was *Nada quita al valiente lo cortez,* which meant that to be courteous even to the most humble never lowered anyone. She practiced what she preached by being kind to all. A friend said once to me: "You don't make enough distinction between yourselves and your servants." My parents were not the haughty kind of Dons; they never made their servants feel that they were inferior. There was no need, for our servants knew their places and kept it.

I loved to watch them at work. *"Comadrita,"* they called me, so kindly. I answered with a silent smile. Only with my mother or someone of my own age did my tongue ever loosen. It was that reverent respect we were taught to have for our elders, more by example than by word, that made us so quiet and restrained in our outer feelings, even among brothers and sisters. *"Hermanita"* — "Little Sister" — all my brothers and my sisters call me even to this day.

Harmony existed always. If father and mother had a different idea about something, they talked it over in a nice way. If mother could not convince my father as to how a thing should be done, she dropped the subject without arguing. When father built the new store extending into the courtyard, she said it would ruin the looks of the house, and it did. It shut out the light from the inside windows. We lost the east inside porch on the court, and with it went my swing that I enjoyed so much, the locust tree and elevated adobe garden around it, where mother grew her old-fashioned marigolds and larkspurs. Around it we had played *monita siega,* blind man's buff. The porch posts we had used for bases in playing at *"las iglesias."*

The outside porch on the east side was also torn down and a new parlor and two bedrooms were built. The family was growing up and we must have more room, and father must have the store where it would be more handy, and not away between the house and the chapel, where my mother wanted it. She saw the attractive side rather that the convenient one. Although the change would save her all the work of having those long porches whitewashed and plastered every year, still she wanted it left in its lovely old style.

We children missed our outdoor sleep. Sometime in very warm weather, mother allowed our maids to take our beds to the inside porch. What fun it was to find our beds by moonlight and to lay there looking up at the starlit heaven! We did not gaze long. After a full day of active work or play, there was no need of sleeping powders for anyone in the family. By nine o'clock every one was ready to drop into dreamland.

CHAPTER IV

Indian Feast of San Geronimo

Great preparations were made several weeks ahead of this the biggest feast, celebrated during the fall, on September 30. It was eagerly looked forward to all the year round, for it brought many visitors from southern Colorado and New Mexico, and homes were filled with guests.

Everybody dressed in new clothes for the occasion. My poor mother, always so willing to help, was greatly imposed upon at this time. Beside seeing to newly outfitting her family of five boys and making me a new dress, relatives would come asking her to help them make over or make a new silk gown. In those days dresses were fancy and lots of work to sew. My father brought mother's gowns ready made, on trips to a city, but mother always was considerate about saving expenses. When the style changed, she would make them over, cutting her paper pattern by a new style one, and had the patience to baste and unbaste seams until the dress fitted perfectly.

For two weeks before the San Geronimo feast day, fierce-looking, filthy Utes trekked slowly over rocky mountain trails from southern Colorado. From the Navajo country in northwestern New Mexico came the aristocratic Navajos, riding better steeds. And the tamed Apaches arrived, seemingly peaceful but with their wild spirit still smouldering, for their lunch. While I was scared of them, still I was curious, and

17

stood on tiptoes behind the counter, by my father's protecting side, to see them. The friendly Picuris, Santa Claras, San Juans, Tesuques and other tribes arrived at Taos from the south. Then followed squeaky wagons and buggies, and horsemen — over lofty hills, down deep arroyos — forming an almost continuous procession descending the steep Arroyo Hondo Hill.

Some of these people took advantage of friendly hospitality and stopped to visit relatives and friends for a few days' rest, after a two or three days' rough journey; others went on to Taos.

On the eve of the feast, wagon after wagon camped overnight under the wild plum trees by the Rio del Pueblo. The smoke of their supper campfires mingled with that of the fires before the tepees of the visiting Indians.

In the pueblo houses, Indian women bearing great water *tinajas* (jars) on their heads climbed steep ladders with grace and poise, and glided softly into their neatly whitewashed rooms. Indian men, resembling oriental Arabs and Egyptians, shrouded in white cotton mantles, stood on the high roofs — white sentinels etched against the blue vault of heaven. Their call was strikingly oriental.

These original Americans were building four-story pueblos, weaving textiles and decorating their simple utensils long before the Spanish colonists discovered this continent. With the dark blue pyramid mountain as background, this pueblo exceeds all other pueblos in beauty of setting and architectural grandeur.

Beyond La Glorieta, picnic grounds of the Taos people, the Indians forbade white people to enter the river canyon. Stories were told about the Indians having a rich gold mine in the mountains, others told of a *biboron* (monster rattlesnake) to which the Indians fed infant babies on certain feast days. This was given as the reason for the non-increase of the pueblo's population.

During the Indian and Spanish uprising against the American occupation, and while the United States soldiers were bombarding the old pueblo church where the natives had fixed their stronghold, the *biboron* was moved to safety from the north pueblo to the south side across the river on a hand-cart covered with blankets. The Indian who braved the shower of missiles in order to save the idol, dropped wounded as he reached the mouth of the kiva. He dragged the monster wrapped in blankets down the ladder, only to drop dead at the bottom of the kiva.

By six o'clock in the morning on September 30, a line of rattling wagons loaded with people had passed by. Buggies, washed and shined, followed on the twelve-mile ride to Taos over the sage-covered plain, to the Arroyo Seco Hill. Below, the Taos valley spread in a broad sweep before the eye, like a checkerboard in green and gold. Wandering south and west, winding streams and irrigation ditches cut their way like shimmering silver ribbons through ripened fields.

Next, the procession crossed El Rio Lucero, named after the morning star because of its crystalline waters. In another hour's ride they had reached El Prado. Attention was drawn to a high round *torrion* (tower), built against the side of the large Spanish-style house owned by Don Jose Isidro Valdez's family. From the inside of this two-story high tower the people in early days fought the Indians, shooting at them through the loopholes at the top.

By now the whole valley was astir. Over all the roads leading to the pueblo were seen all kinds of conveyances and men on horseback, raising great clouds of dust. At the north entrance of the pueblo, etched against the purple mountain and unspotted blue sky, stood part of the front wall and high tower of the ruins of the old pueblo church, destroyed during the Indian revolution in 1847. Crumbling adobes and broken roof beams lay in heaps, as on the day of the battle.

The carriages drove on and parked on both sides of the racetrack. And from the covered wagons camped under the shade of the cottonwood trees by the river came the fruit vendors, carrying in their arms willow baskets piled high with luscious black grapes, rosy peaches and pears and melons

19

brought from the warm lands of El Rio Abajo. It did not take them long to dispose of their loads among the assembled country people. Children greedily devoured the fruit, for this treat came to them only once a year. They paid little heed to the ringing of the chapel bell and to the procession which moved from the church to a shrine built of tree branches on top of a *tapeiste*.

The Inditas, carrying the statue of San Geronimo, the patron saint of their parish, climbed the ladder and placed the statue in the shrine. Below stood a semi-circle of young Indian men swaying, their nude bodies painted in patches of green, yellow, and white, with red ochre around their eyes and on their temples. Yucca was tied to their ankles for speed, and colored feathers were stuck in their hair. They were now ready for the relay race, the big event of the day. Two of the young Indians, one from each pueblo, started down the track; two others ran from the opposite end of the quarter-mile course. Along the race course — about four hundred yards in length — stood old Indian chiefs wrapped in bright-colored blankets. Others were dressed in beaded chamois, strings of bright feathers circling their heads and hanging down to their heels. Becoming excited when their runners fell a lap or two behind the opponents, these old men would yell excitedly, "Ha-ma-pah, pu-lu-lu," and hit the heels of the racers with aspen branches as they sped by.

After the races, the chiefs and drum men encircled the runners. Then, singing, dancing, and rustling golden aspen tree branches to beat of the drum, they slowly moved to the victor's pueblo, where Indian squaws, dressed in gorgeous colored silks and flowered shawls, came out on the terraced roofs with baskets full of *tortillas* and biscuits. They dropped these down to the victors, a gesture significant of the abundance of the harvest. In every house was a feast spread for visiting tribes and friends. The fields were turned into free pasture, and the sweet, wild plums were gathered freely.

For color, this feast is unrivaled in New Mexico. The northside pueblo, at the foot of the mountain, at this time of the year is in gorgeous alpine autumn colors. The pueblo fields are covered with yellow sunflowers, green and yellow pumpkins and wild plum trees decorated with bright red and yellow fruit. The terraced pueblo roofs are solid masses of people and Indians in bright silk and satin dresses. The golden aspen tree branches carried by the Indians and decorating the shrine, the vendor's fruit baskets — all mingle in a riot of color.

In a cloud of dust the crowd of people left the pueblo and poured into the usually sleepy town of Don Fernando, which suddenly awoke to make ready every available room in hotel and home to home the arriving throng. The ancient town, made famous in New Mexico's history by the names of Governor Bent and Kit Carson, famous scout, still preserved the appearance of the old dwellings of the days of the *conquistadores*. It was a bit of old Spain mingled with a touch of Anglo and French left there by the American troops and Canadian trappers. The Pueblo Indians always in the plaza added another touch to the romantic background of this interesting place.

In the afternoon, the crowd flocked back to the pueblo to see the "chifonetes" Indian Koshares perform their clownish stunts. Out of the kivas came the clowns, their nude bodies and faces grotesquely painted. They clambered over walls and into wagons, frightening children and provoking the women and the girls with their mirth-provoking tricks. After they had amused the crowd for a time, they discovered the smooth-shaved, greased pole standing in the yard. With miniature bows and arrows they tried to bring down the fat lamb, watermelon and bundle of biscuits tied at the top of the pole. Then they decided to climb the pole and get them. After many unsuccessful attempts, two or three of them formed a line on the pole, each pushing the foremost one with his head. The top of the pole, in this manner, was reached without difficulty. A rope was tossed to the topmost clown, and by that means the sheep and bundles were lowered, to be divided among the clan.

After witnessing this fun-making, the crowd went back to the plaza of Don Fernando de Taos, where the Spanish

21

part of the fiesta was in full swing. In three or four *salas, fandangos* were going on. Musicians had come from other towns, rivaling each other in displaying their talents; and the dancers visited one hall after another, the largest and best crowd finally settling in the one that had the best music. The dances continued for three nights, until the third of October, when the crowd moved over to Ranchos, to celebrate vespers on the eve of the feast of San Francisco.

This feast started the round of *fiestas* throughout the valley. Los Cordovas, Rio Chiquito, La Loma — each in turn celebrated its patron saint's feast. La Loma celebrated the feast of Saint Anthony on the third of November, although this saint's feast day came on June 13. But in the spring, people did not have time for feasting.

Later in the fall, my mother took the family one evening to see the *mielero,* where the cane syrup was being made. There was a great deal of hustle and bustle around the yard and the primitive mud stove built against the wall of the house. It was fun to watch the boys fight and scramble for a ride on the *viga prenza.* The seesawing of the viga lifted and let down the press in the barrel, squeezing the juice out of the cane. The juice ran out through a hole into a wooden trough, was put into earthen jars with a gourd dipper and the pots set to boil on the mud stove until it was a clear red, then strained and poured into earthen jars.

Another night we went to a puppet show, *"Titeres."* A Mexican that came into town gave the show in a large room. Most of the audience sat on the wool-carpeted floor in front of the table, as seats were scarce. A kerosene lamp set in a wall niche dimly lit the table on which the rag dolls were deftly operated by the man behind the black curtain. He gave us four amusing acts.

Another time a Mexican traveling troupe gave us a very good performance right in our enclosed courtyard. The man and woman were skilled acrobats, and I marveled at their tricks on the trapeze. The *pallacito,* boy clown, was most witty and entertaining with his amusing jokes. Another

INDIAN FEAST OF SAN GERONIMO

traveling show gave a *panorama* of five colored pictures on a white sheet screen. One 4th of July my father sprang on us a new treat which thrilled us and the valley people — shooting colored fireworks.

Arab gypsies in their picturesque garb passed through selling trinkets, making the poor people believe that the rosaries and medals had been blest in one of Blessed Mary's dishes in Nazareth. The good people bought their trinkets, and fed the gypsies.

The *convites* and *gallos* that passed along the streets with music, inviting the people to these shows and to dances, broke up the quiet, and enlivened everyone, especially on the feast day dances. In this way we did not lack entirely entertainment.

CHAPTER V

The Parish Feast Day

"Often happy feasts brightened the day,
When toil forgetting,
The village people turned to play;
Led up to ancient sports,
That pleased in peaceful sorts."

During late fall and early winter was the only time when
real rest came, and it was doubly enjoyed, earned at a high
price.

The work finished, and mud granaries filled to the brim
with precious grain, ripe pumkins, dried fruits and vegetables that had been stored away, the people turned to play
and feasting.

Marriages and religious feasts were solemnized. Races and
sport games were held.

The first celebration was the parish patron saint's feast
day. It opened with the accustomed vespers on the eve before, and high mass next morning. There were no seats in
the church. Our nurse walked in ahead of mother and spread
the wool *tilma* on the floor, wherever her mistress chose to
kneel.

The church did not have an organ. The priest brought
with him from Taos the French singer, and Miguel accompanied the singing with his fiddle. Refreshments were served
at the *mayordomo's* home for those who dropped in.

24

THE PARISH FEAST DAY

In the afternoon, different sports or dances were held. The Matachines dance was sometimes given in the open plaza square, and from there the dancers came up the *cordillera* and gave our family a treat performance in our yard. They got treated also.

The villages, usually dark at night, were lit up and lively, for the *mayordomo* was giving a dance, the closing event of the fiesta.

The women used the high window sills as dressing tables, resting their mirrors against their oil lamps while they applied the red carmine to their cheeks and the white *albayalde* to their faces and necks with their fingertips. With hair dressed up high and a few flat ringlets pasted with sugar on their foreheads and the high-bustled dresses donned, the *doñas* and *señoritas* were ready to be escorted to the dance.

Oil lamps and board floors were already in use in my village, but in some of the more remote villages the dance hall was illuminated by candles placed on two crossed sticks hanging from the ceiling, and the mud floor was sprinkled with water between dances to keep the dust down.

The *bastonero* called out the dances and picked out from the crowd of men standing by the door the ones who were to take part in each dance, by this means avoiding crowding. At weddings and other invitation dances this was not necessary. The niceties of courtesty were still observed. In inviting a lady to a dance, the man bowed before her. Offering his arm, he escorted her to the center of the hall to stand in line with the other ladies. The men stood also in line before their partners until the music started.

My parents, being so popular, were very often invited by the elite to stand as sponsors at baptisms and as attendants at weddings. My mother dressed the bride so tastily, and she herself looked so lovely in her fine silk or velvet gowns and fine jewels, I was always at her side silently admiring and learning, happy to go when she chose to take me and contented to stay if she chose to leave me at home.

The harmonious relations among the villagers were perpetuated not only by intermarriages among the same family

25

relatives, but also by this considered spiritual relation of *compadres* brought on by sponsoring their children.

The season of repose had come, and while the land rested under a blanket of snow, the farmers sought diversion in sports and games.

After the gay young men left on their buffalo hunt, and others in caravans, the village settled down into dormancy.

White-bearded men with hard-lined faces sat on their haunches, resting their tired backs against the sunny walls, fully occupied with cracking *piñon* nuts and quietly discussing the last county election or *fiesta*.

On a large level field across the river, on bright Sunday afternoons, the more active men played *el juego de pelota*. When the upper town men played against the lower town team, the ball was brought down through the fields, a distance of two miles. A hot struggle carried the ball back and forth until one of the sides succeeded in hitting the fence marked as the winning goal. The losers paid by giving a dance.

Horse races took place out on the level *llanito*. The men bet money, the women, *surdarios* and *rosarios*.

In sunny *placitas*, men gathered to witness cock fights. For weeks before the fight, the roosters were fed and given special care. Heavy wagers made the sport exciting.

When not engaged in sports or exciting games, the men played *el hoyo* and moved with the sun to snow-cleared patios. Two small, round holes were dug in the ground about thirty feet apart. Each player, standing by one of the holes, took two turns at throwing his *tejas* (flat, round stones about three inches in diameter) into the opposite hole. Three points were won with each *teja* that fell inside the hole, one or two points by the ones that fell on the edge or touched the hole. Sometimes the next player knocked his opponent's *teja* into the hole, which counted three points for him.

Through the long, winter evenings, neighbors gathered before warm fireplaces to play *cañute*, card games, and to tell interesting stories. My mother also found time to relax.

THE PARISH FEAST DAY

While resting, she told us beautiful stories. Twenty-five of these stories I translated into English and had them published in my book of *Spanish Fairy Tales*. Tiodora, our nurse, told us some creepy, ghost and witch stories and when we children were not very good she would call *orejas de burro* or the *vieja ganchos* to her aid. The *burro* would stick his long donkey ears through a crack in the door, and the *vieja* would appear crouching at the door, showing us her long hook. My cry would suddenly catch in my throat. Immediately there was perfect quiet. But oh! those awful dreams, in which I saw myself being carried out to the mountains hanging from the *vieja ganchos'* hook. I would wake up stiff with fright. I believe now that these awful stories, the fear of the *abuelos,* and the sore example put before us of bad children like the *mal hijo,* made our lives exceedingly repressed.

Stories about miraculous cures that happened at the Santuario at Chimayo I thought very wonderful, and even some of the cures by the *medicas* were not far short of miracles. One was by old Refugio, the *medica.* Her daughter, Josefa, developed *pupas,* a bad sore on her upper lip. It ate into her cheek and tongue. Refugio washed the sores with blue *piedralipe* that the farmers use to cure smut on wheat. The sores healed. Lupe, the sister, caught the same disease. She did not have the courage to try the cure. She had seen how her sister raved with the pain, night and day, when she used the wash. The disease ate through to her throat, and poor Lupe, unable to swallow any food, soon succumbed to it. Thinking I had found a cure for cancer, I told Dr. Masie about it, but he called their ailment some other disease. Another cure was on Benito. He had suffered with a terrible pain in the stomach. Doctors pronounced it cancer, and gave him only a few more weeks to live. But a mother never gives up to the last. She called a *medica.* With massages and physics the *medica* dislodged the hard lump, *empacho,* and it was expelled with excruciating pain. Benito regained his health and weight and is a strong young man today. These are only two examples, but there were many more cures performed by just simple remedies.

CHAPTER VI

English Teaching Schools

The Santa Fe diocese then in United States territory, four years after its annexation, the Rev. Baptist Lamy was sent to Santa Fe to take charge of the diocese as vicar-apostolic. A few years after he was elevated to archbishop. An authentic picture of his noble, energetic life is given in Willa Cather's book, *Death Comes for the Archbishop.*

The smart vicar saw at once how sadly neglected education had been and set to work to remedy it. He brought from the East, Jesuits, Christian brothers and Loretto nuns. St. Michael's College and Loretto School were established. Later another Loretto Convent School was opened in Taos. Spanish teaching public schools had been estabilshed in 1721 by order of the Spanish king. Later energetic Governor Mariano Martinez had two professors come from Spain, and he himself, with his own money, helped carry on the work of teaching. Padre José Antonio Martinez in 1826 had established a college in Taos at his own expense.

My father had attended St. Michael's College a few years and had learned English fairly well. He was able to give traveling salesmen orders for his store, and became very friendly with some of the Americans in Taos.

Now he sent my oldest brother to this same school in Santa Fe. I was just eight years old and was tutored in Cousin Inocencio's private school that year. At the closing exercises, two of us little girls recited the little dialogue of "Luisa and Maria's Lost Thimble." I was very proud of my Spanish recitation. The next year I passed the Mantilla's Spanish Second Reader, which graduated me at this school. One cold November morning, wrapped in a wool robe, I sat comfortably seated between my father and mother, riding to Don Fernando de Taos. It was one of those bright mornings when New Mexico sunshine caused the snowclad mountains and wide plains to sparkle as if covered with diamonds. We enjoyed the beautiful sight and the brisk cold air for two hours before we reached the town. My father drove the team through the convent side gate close to the building, to get my trunk down.

A blonde girl and a nun came out to meet us. The girl, Alice, picked me up from the buggy seat and carried me in. "I didn't want you to get your pretty white shoes muddy," she said, setting me down on the parlor carpet. I had insisted on wearing the high-buttoned white shoes my father had bought me in the summer. I noticed the nuns looked down at them with a critical eye, and I felt a little sorry mother had humored me in letting me wear white shoes in the winter.

Sister Rosana, the principal, came in and told Alice to take me into the recreation room with the other girls. I didn't even know when my parents left. I at once became happily acquainted, as two of the boarders, Ciria and Juanita, where my cousins. Being the baby of the school, I right away became the favorite with the nuns and with Alice, who insisted on waiting on me.

"You are so little and your hair is so soft. I love to comb it," she would say, holding me on her lap while brushing my hair. Sister Tiotiste called me her little *Piñon*. We were not allowed to speak any Spanish, and the first English words were, "Put some wood in the stove."

Sister LaKostka always took me as her companion when she went on her business errands to town. Sometimes we rode out to the country villages looking for more boarders or soliciting for donations. These were red-letter days for me.

ROMANCE OF A LITTLE VILLAGE GIRL

Among the day-schoolers were decendants of prominent pioneer families. They were an interesting blend of nationalities and traditions left, during Taos' stormy days, first by the Spanish colonists, then by the Americans and French and the Indians who were already rooted there.

Dora and Mercedes Sherrick were Governor Bent's granddaughters. Others were half-French Clothiers, Bobians, German Jews. The two daughters of Alex Gusdorf, the enterprising merchant, who opened the first store at Ranchos, planted the first fruit orchard, brought the first threshing machine into the valley, opened the first steam-run flour mill. His flour mill became a very productive industry. Beside supplying the valley, he also furnished flour to two army posts. After each harvest, several wagons were at my father's garnary door early in the morning to haul the wheat that Mr. Gusdorf bought to the mill.

With only six boarders and about fifty day pupils, the nuns made a scanty living. Every summer at the close of school they would threaten that they were not coming back. At once some of the people interested in giving their childdren a Christian education would get busy and persuade the school board to give the nuns the public school in town. Thus the nuns would return in September to reopen the school, and we few boarders would be back again. Each year I felt more at home. I loved the nuns and had a reverent respect for them, and was happiest at my school work. I was especially fond of art and fancy work of all kinds.

On Saturdays we did our mending and took our bath, in a wash tub placed behind a screen in one corner of the recreation room. In the afternoon, I could hardly wait to get to the art room, where dear Sister Cleotilde taught me to paint and embroider. How I loved to handle the pretty shaded silk chenille and sparkling gold and silver tinsel, with which I emboidered sprays of flowers, birds and butterflies on velvet scarves and cushions. My mother was so proud of my work she had my last piece framed for the parlor. From soft, delicate shaded wax sheets I cut flower petals, made roses, pansies, fuchsias, sprays of dainty forget-me-nots and green leaves, arranged them in pretty moss-filled baskets and carried them ever so carefully on my lap, to present to mother at Easter.

Sister Rosana must have noticed the great thirst I had for learning, for she took special interest in teaching me piano herself. One day she called me into her office and sat me by her while she taught me how to knit a pink wool bonnet. When it was finished she helped me line it with pink silk. I surely was grateful to her when I wore it to church on cold mornings. She also took interest in my health. Sister LaKostka must have reported to her how little I ate at the table, for she called me in to see Dr. Martin, just newly-arrived, young and handsome. He said I had dyspepsia and put me on an iron tonic. I knew it was that awful meat and potato hash and pork headcheese that upset my appetite. This was our daily supper.

On this, my first year at school, my father called to take me home Christmas Eve. The nuns were shocked, knowing that I would be missing mass on this great feast day as we did not have a resident priest in our village.

As we descended the last ridge of the hill at the end of our cold ride, the last rays of the sinking sun turned the highest mountain peaks a glowing rose. The snow lay heavily in the deep valley of the Arroyo Hondo, half burying the silent little villages. When we arrived, mother sent me into her room to thaw out my half-frozen feet before the fire. "She didn't tell me she was cold," my father told mother. No, I had not complained; I always took discomforts as part of life, nothing to make a fuss over.

Erineo was clearing the snow off our frontyard when we arrived, and my brothers were carrying the pitchwood sticks with which to build the *luminarias*. As the deepening shadows of night spread over the valley, the red glow of these bonfires lit the whole front of our house and all through the village brightened the little adobe houses and warmed the men and boys standing around them.

Inside our house, there was great activity in the kitchen.

31

ROMANCE OF A LITTLE VILLAGE GIRL

The children warmed the *piñon* nuts and shelled them by rubbing them between two boards. These nuts and cleaned raisins went into the mince meat filling in the little fried pies. These *empanaditas* and fried *sopaipias* were passed to the *oremo* boys who came to the kitchen door reciting carols.

Lupe, our Indian cook, and Tiodora, the nurse, prepared the dough, and mother helped them make the tamales to be served for the Christmas breakfast. I made *chapitos* for those who could not eat the tamales with chile. These I stuffed with cheese and raisins. How white, light and fluffy the tamales were, so different from those served at restaurants. In my cook book, *Potajes Sabrosos,* I give the right recipe for how to make them.

Down in the village chapel the wake of the Holy Child was held, and sometimes the shepherd play was given. A group of actors, led by the couple representing Mary and Joseph going through the streets in Bethlehem seeking shelter for the night, went from house to house until they were admitted. Refreshments then were passed to them.

In my second school year, my father did not come to take me home until Christmas morning. Santa Claus was still unknown to us in those days, and when the nun told us his story, it filled me with so much wonder I was glad I had stayed to find out more about this mystic man. Before leaving for the midnight mass, the three boarders remaining at the convent hung our stockings in the recreation room. That long mass in the ice-cold church seemed endless. At last we were back in the recreation room digging into our stockings, bringing out a stick candy, a red apple and fried *sopaipa.* This tasted as good as cake after that cold walk. I went to bed to dream of good Santa Claus. This was a happier dream than the ones about the stern old *abuelo* who dressed in a shabby, patched suit and went around the *luminarias* cracking his long whip and scaring the boys to go home and say their prayers. But no sooner was he out of sight than the boys were out again running and jumping over the dying bonfires.

On New Year's Day, music was heard early in the morning as the fiddlers went through the village serenading all persons named Manuel. When the door of the house was opened, the host was greeted with a little verse. The serenaders were invited in and treated with refreshments.

The day after New Year's I was back at school with some little trinket some relative had given me as a present. My other two cousins were also back. Cousin Ciria's mother had been a widow several years when she shocked the family by marrying her uncle, my Grandpa Lucero. Her excuse was that my mother's father was the only man she knew who came near being as good a man as her first husband.

We children were too old to change, and kept on calling her Aunt Piedad. She was one of the Gallegos women, famous for their beauty. She was truly a handsome woman. Tall, heavy-set, with fair complexion, black eyes, and an abundance of hair such as I have never seen on another head except in pictures of the three sisters advertising hair shampoo. Grandpa had good taste; his first wife had also been a very noted beauty. Aunt Piedad was the symbol of those days that have passed, when the ladies had a gracious living, having been brought up in the tradition of refined helplessness, to be waited on. She lived a leisurely life with her three daughters in her attractive home. Her pride was giving pleasure to them — buying them fine clothes, a fine carriage in which, after their siesta, the house servant took them on a ride, visiting, coming back in time to sit at a nice supper Juana had already prepared for them. In the evening we played games of *canute,* or she told us pretty stories, and then she had the whole family kneel, including servants, while she recited in her full voice the longest night prayers.

Across the road from her big house, my aunt had the cutest three-story summer house. It contained three rooms, one above the other, surrounded by white porches, and with a narrow stairway leading up to each story. The rooms were furnished with small couches and chairs in walnut. Pretty flower scenes, in old-fashioned frames, adorned the walls. Below the back porch, white ducks swam in the artificial lake.

33

To one of the back porch posts was tied a small boat, ready for the girls to put out for a row on the lake.

After her second marriage, my grandfather built a new thirteen-room house in the square Spanish style, with the hollow square surrounded with white porches. The parlor in front was furnished with expensive upholstered furniture and rich carpets. Two very fine Saltillo *sarapes* had been ripped apart and fringed to serve as side drapes for the fine lace curtains. A beautiful hanging lamp, gold candle sticks with crystal pendants, and other lovely ornaments added richness to the room.

Invitations were sent out for the housewarming party and dance, which was held in the long new storeroom. Since I was so chummy with Cousin Ciria, my parents took me to the party. We reached Taos in the evening in time to join mother's friend, Mrs. Sherrick, and her three daughters, who were also going to the party. Aunt Piedad looked more handsome then ever in her fine silk taffeta gown, wearing her fine pearls. This was an affair never to be forgotten, as were my visits to this home on weekends, when my grandfather took Cousin Ciria and me there. Sister Rosana always instructed him to return us on Sunday evening, but grandpa, being one of the kind Luceros, after a few beggings would let us stay until Monday morning. "And what will you pay me?" he would ask. We always promised him something good — a cake or cookies — but the debt was never paid.

34

CHAPTER VII

Penitente Ceremonies of Holy Week

For the four-day Easter vacation, my father again took me home to Arroyo Hondo. The Holy Week religious ceremonies were very different from what these are now.

In our hidden nook, isolated from the outside world and still untouched by modern progress, people were content to live their simple lives. Religion was the most important thing to them. Still holding to ceremonies carried on from the medieval age of faith and religious traditions, during lent every year they reenacted with sincere religious fervor the sorrows of the Passion Play. The *penitente* brotherhood took charge of the religious ceremonies, inasmuch as there was no resident priest in the town in my time.

On Monday and Tuesday of Holy Week the conical adobe ovens were seen smoking throughout the three villages while the week's supply of bread and *panocha* was being baked. The mud ovens must be blessed before using them, or they won't bake the bread right; to bless the oven, a cross is laid on the floor of the oven, salt is sprinkled on the cross and prayers recited.

At the *penitentes' morada,* where half the male population congregated on Wednesday, one *mayordomo* (or sometimes two) was chosen for each day to supply the food for the brothers, who fasted from Wednesday morning until Saturday noon. The *mayordomos* vied with each other in

35

treating the *hermanos* to the nicest repast. Four or five of the *acompanadores* (brethren of light) were seen coming out of the *mayordomo's* house carrying four copper kettles hanging on a stick. These kettles contained *torrejas con chile* (egg fritters in chile sauce), *rueditas* (fried dried squash), and *sopa de fideos* (home made spaghetti). In an earthen bowl they carried bread pudding with cheese and raisins. All meat was forbidden during the four holy days. Recipes for these lenten dishes will be found in my cook book of Spanish recipes.

There was a great deal of exchanging done of *charolitas,* dishes, at noon on both Holy Thursday and Good Friday. Neighbors and friends were seen carrying back and forth small bowls filled with *panocha, capirotada, torejas,* or whatever other nice dish they had prepared.

The *morada* stood across the river, a few yards below the town. On each side of the door, resting against the wall, was a pile of century-old crosses which were kept inside the secret room from year to year.

With a field glass my family had a very good view of the *penitentes* as they came out of the *morada.* The members were told that with this field glass we could distinguish their faces through the black masks. After this, for fear of being detected, the brethren of light stood in line outside the front of the door, holding up outspread blankets, thus screening the *penitentes* while they came out. The *penitentes* took up their crosses, and a blanket was thrown over them, leaving only their heads and feet exposed. Followed by the *hermanos de deciplina* (flagellants), they dragged their heavy crosses around to the back of the *morada* and proceeded on their painful way up the rocky trail to *El Calvario* (Calvary Cross on the hill).

On *Viernes de Dolores,* the Friday before Good Friday, my grandmother carried out her votive promise of giving an alm and a dinner to the poorest family in the village.

She had brought from old Mexico her favorite painting of *Nuestra Señora de Los Dolores* (Our Lady of Sorrows).

PENITENTE CEREMONIES OF HOLY WEEK

The beauitful madonna face, with a tear like a pearl rolling down her pink cheek and her hands clasping tightly the handle of the sword piercing her heart under her blue mantle, was tinted in soft shades on a tin sheet and framed in a fancy tin frame. Throughout the year every dime or nickel that the grandchildren could save was pasted around the picture inside the glass covering it.

The daughters and their children were invited also to the dinner. At the end of the meal, the tin frame with the painting was brought down; the nickels and dimes were taken off, and together with a crown made from coffee cake dough, the hollow center filled with *melcochas* candies, was given to the poor family as the promised alm.

Moved by curiosity, I once asked a *penitente's* wife who was going to pay a votive promise to the *santos* at the *morada* if I might accompany her. We climbed the hill on which the *morada* stood in the upper town and were admitted to the chapel. On the wall of the hall dividing the chapel from the secret room hung a row of palm whips. The woman crawled on her knees from one statue to another, placing lighted candles before each. I was left kneeling before the statue of the Crucifixion. Paralyzed with fear, I could not move, for there before me on the mud altar table stood the statue of Death staring at me with one glass eye, the other eye shut, aiming at me with her drawn bow and arrow. Behind me I heard the *hermanos* going in and out of the room. I did not dare turn around for fear of seeing a *penitente* standing in back of me. This visit satisfied my curiosity.

For a couple of years during Holy Week a flagellant *penitente* with his *acompanador* came to our private chapel and asked permission to go in and make a visit. While the brother of light recited the prayers, the brother lay prostrated with arms extended on the floor before the altar. He got up and stood by the door while flogging himself, and then passed in front of our store on the way back to the *morada*. My family persisted in believing that this was the man who helped himself to one of the fat lambs from our corral and had come to atone for it. The ofen-repeated verse of *"Penitente peca-*

dor, porque te andas azotando? Porque me comi un carnero gordo y ahora lo hando desquitando," applied in this case.

On one occasion, hearing the doleful notes of the *penitentes'* flute, I ran out to the front porch in time to see three *penitentes de madero* passing on their way to visit the lower town *morada.* My uncle, sitting on the porch step, teasingly grabbed me by both hands and swung me out towards them. My breath caught with fright as I thought that one of them had stretched out his hand from under his blanket to grab my feet.

Anyone wishing to see a *penitente* now must stay up quite late at night, and then he may get only a glimpse, as they come out only one or two at a time and are very carefully guarded and screened by the *acompanadores.*

On Maundy Thursday at two o'clock in the afternoon, *the Emprendimiento* (Seizure of Christ) took place. Men carrying the statue of *Nuestro Padre Jesus,* a life-sized statue of Jesus of Nazareth, crowned with thorns and dressed in a long red tunic, led the procession out of the church. The *resador,* reading the seizure and trial of Christ, walked behind the statue, followed by the throng of women.

From *la morada* on the opposite side of the town two files of brethren of light, representing the Jews, started out. These men had red handkerchiefs tied over their heads with a knot on top representing a helmet. They were preceded by a man dressed like a centurion. The Jews carried long iron chains and *matracas,* or rattlers. On meeting the procession coming from the church, they stopped before the statue and asked, "Who art Thou?" The men carrying the statue answered. *"Jesus El Nacareno* (Jesus of Nazareth)." The Jews then seized the statue, tied the statue's hands with a white cord, while their leader read the arrest sentence. The other Jews stood loudly clanging the chains and rattling the *matracas.* They led the procession back to the *morada,* carrying with them the statue.

El Incuentro. The next morning — Good Friday — the same two groups took part in the ceremony. This time the group that left the church carried the statue of *Nuestra Señora de La Soledad* (The Sorrowful Mary), dressed in black, a blank mantle covering her head, over which a silver halo shone. The procession of men representing the Jews came from the *morada* carrying the statue of Christ. The two groups met halfway around the town, representing the meeting of Christ and His Mother. One of the women took a white cloth from her head, and approaching on her knees wiped the face of the statue, while the grieving Marys wept real tears aloud. The *resador* read the passage of the meeting of Christ and His Mother as the procession walked back to the church.

About half an hour later, *La Procesion de Sangre* (the bloody procession of all the *penitentes* combined, in a long double file of flagellants) was seen winding its way up the rocky trail to the *Calvario*, then back again to the *morada*. Special self-imposed penances were practiced between one and three o'clock in the afternoon. A lone *penitente* sometimes staggered up the trail surrounded by brethren of light. He dragged his feet tied with a heavy iron chain. On his back a bunch of sharp cactus needles pricked his flesh at every step.

Good Friday. *Las Tres Caidas* (The Three Falls). The largest and heaviest cross was picked out and laid upon the shoulder of the *hermano* who chose to represent the crucified Christ. A crown of thorns was placed on his head, and a bunch of prickly cactus was hung on his back. Laboriously, the *penitente* dragged the scraping cross up the rocky trail. Two brethren of light walked on each side of him, one reading the three falls in the Stations of the Cross from an open book in his hand. The other, acting the part of Simon Cyrene, helped the *hermano* lift the weighty cross when he stumbled and fell under its weight. A group of brethren of light had already dug a pit and gathered a pile of rocks by Calvary cross. The stood around the *Calvario*, awaiting the *Cristo* brother, who, on reaching the hill, was stretched upon his cross and tied with ropes. The cross was raised and placed in the pit surrounded by the pile of rocks to hold it upright.

39

The *hermanos* knelt with bowed heads around the cross, praying and reciting the Seven Last Words of the crucified Savior. The voice of the man upon the cross grew more and more faint, as he repeated the words, until his body hung limp, and he was taken down and carried on a blanket, too weak to carry his cross back to the *morada*.

Las Estaciones. At three o'clock the people gathered at the church for the Stations of the Cross. The procession of *penitentes,* some carrying crosses and others switching their lacerated backs, came first. Between the two files walked a masked *penitente* pulling a small cart in which stood the statue of Death. The *acompanador,* walking behind the cart, now and then picked up a large stone and dropped it into the cart to make it heavier to pull. The men carrying the statue of *Nuestro Padre Jesus,* another man with a crucifix, and the reader walked in the center of the procession. As the *resador* read each station of the cross, the people knelt on the ground, then arose and walked singing a verse of the *alabado de las columnas.*

Alabado

En una columna atado,	Onto a pillar,
Estaba El Rey del Cielo.	The King of Heaven was tied.

Chorus

Herido y ensangrentado	Wounded and bloody,
Y arrastrado por los suelos	He was dragged on the ground.

A few days after the close of Holy Week, some of the young men would appear at the store looking pale and haggard. My brother, curious to find out if a certain young man were a *penitente,* gave him a friendly slap on the back. Taken unawares, the man betrayed his secret by a painful shrug and expression of agony on his face. The aim of the confraternity was evident in their lives. Their law was to live in peace and in the charity of Christ, prayer to be their support in all their afflictions. Those who were sincere to their rules were religious and scrupulous.

Sabado de Gloria closed the Holy Week with joy and cheer, for lent ended at noon on Holy Saturday, and a big ball was given that night.

In most of the old Spanish mansions a *sala* (long living room) was always included. In this room the private invitation dances were given. To these dances only the exclusive Spanish society was invited. *Carestrolendas,* egg shells filled with confetti or cologne water, were taken to the dances. These were playfully broken on the heads of the dancers, providing much merriment. Refreshments of wine, *biscochitos,* cakes and candies were passed to all the guests. This custom of a ball on Saturday was attacked by the towns' parish priests in their sermons, but in the remote villages which the priest visited only once a month the people followed their own rules and customs.

A rich folklore was found among the natives, in their customs and superstitions. These included mystic stories which the *penitentes'* families were made to believe in order to keep their flagellant practices secret. The *penitentes* were souls that God permitted to come back from the other world to finish making reparation for their sins. They were heard sometimes in dark churches flogging themselves and were out in the hills at night carrying crosses or flogging.

On Easter Monday, the usual class work and religious practices were resumed.

About the end of June, the school closed with no other ceremony than goodby to the nuns and school chums.

My father again awaited me in the convent parlor. My favorite Sister Clotilde went out to the carriage with us. I felt sad at parting. We had so much fun working together in the art room and planting the flower bed under the recreation room window.

I climbed up on the seat by my father and rode along inhaling the fresh fragrance of the newly-awakened sage and wild flowers. The desert plain seemed turned into a fairy-land. Icy winter had given place to warm summer, melting snow and filling rivers and causing ditches to overflow. Here and there we dropped into a verdant little valley, the spark-ling river fringed with new green plants and drooping wil-lows. From the edge of the highest ridge we looked down into the Arroyo Hondo sunken valley, which in its rich ver-dure seemed to lie asleep, the deep silence enveloping the valley broken only by the rattling of our carriage wheels or the distant barking of a dog. Happy in letting my tongue loose in my fond Spanish, I had chatted all the way.

We arrived home in time for the feast of St. John. The women and children were up early on the twenty-fourth of June. At six o'clock they were bathing in the river and ditches; small children were splashing cold water at each other. The waters in the streams were believed to be holy on this day, and better health awaited those who bathed at least their face and feet, for St. John baptized Jesus in the Jordan and blessed the waters.

The day was kept as a rogation day. By eight o'clock in the morning a procession started from the church in the upper town. Standing on a platform, the pretty statue of Our Lady of the Rosary, dressed in gala tunic, and the statue of St. John, carried in the arms of one of his devotees, were taken on a tour through the fields to the lower village. On arriving there the procession started visiting each house. A boy beating a drum went ahead announcing the approach of the procession, which halted a few feet from the door. The lady of the house came out to meet the *santos* with a little earthen tray full of live coals; over this she sprinkled aroma-tic incense, incensed the statues and helped carry them in, and placed them on an improvised altar decorated with wild flowers and greens. Around the altar the group knelt, while the lady recited some prayers, sang a hymn and pinned a flower or jewel on Our Lady's gown. Having visited every house, the procession proceeded on its way to the next village and up the *cordillera* to the upper town church. Here the wake was held that night at the church.

PENITENTE CEREMONIES OF HOLY WEEK

The national patron saint of Spain was and still is celebrated in some of the northern towns, on the twenty-fifth of July. He is St. James, and the day is the Feast of Santiago. After the morning services at the church, the statue of St. James, the patron saint of *los caballeros* (horsemen), was carried in procession through the town. Two files of gallant horsemen, *socios de Santiago,* their horses' bridles decorated with flowers and flags, rode ahead of the procession. A few yards from the procession they halted, turned and rode back through the center of the procession in pairs to meet the statue. The two files crossed and galloped ahead. Again they whirled and galloped back to the statue, repeating this during the whole procession.

The *gallo* race, held years ago, has been replaced by horse races and modern sports. The rooster race of old was similar to the rooster race the Indians have at San Juan Pueblo, except that the Mexicans, instead of hanging the rooster as the Indians do, bury it in the ground, leaving its head exposed.

At Arroyo Hondo a group of *galleros* gathered at one end of the street, about fifty feet from the buried cock. One by one, they raced past the rooster, back and forth at full speed, leaning over the side of their saddles to grapple at the fowl, until one of them succeeded in grabbing its head and unearthing it. Swinging it by the legs over his head with a triumphant shout, he spurred his horse and raced ahead, the whole pack of horsemen yelling and racing after him. Up the *cordillera* they chased to the upper town. When finally one of the *galleros* overtook him, he turned and hit the man with the rooster. The challenged horseman grabbed away the trophy and raced ahead, hotly pursued by the others. The rooster changed hands in this way several times during the race. Back they came like an avalanche, lashing their horses, yelling and racing down the hill to the lower town, where they crowded around the leader. A hot skirmish ensued. The *gallero* defended himself by striking in all directions with the rooster, until the cock was torn to pieces.

After several roosters met this cruel fate, the crowd scat-

43

tered, and a wagon was hitched, in which the *convite* for the *baile* started out. A fiddler, a guitarist and a singer climbed into the wagon and rode around the three towns, playing and singing, finally coming back to the hall where the dance was to be held. This was the public invitation to the dance.

Early in the evening the hall was packed. Gray-haired *abuelitas* cuddling the *nietos* lined the back row around the hall. The young women who took part in the dances sat in front. All classes mingled in these public dances, from the silk-gowned *patrona* to the calico-dressed Indian maid. Some of the old-fashioned dances were still danced. The elite left the dance early, before the men became too gay with drinks. Sometimes a drunkard forced his way into the hall, causing great excitement when the *bastonero* tried to push him out. Jealous husbands and lovers sometimes took advantage of the commotion to get even with their rivals, and a fist fight took place in the middle of the hall. The women — screaming and jumping over seats, dragging by the hand children that were half asleep — pushed their way out. When finally the *bastonero,* with the aid of the sheriff or sober men, restored order, the dance went on.

Through the clouds of smoke from the home-grown *punche* tobacco cigarettes, the bent heads and crouching shoulders of the *musicos* were seen. There was languor and softness in the wire strings, then recklessness and madness, as the dance wore on and *tragitos* from the musicians' pocket flasks went up to their heads.

Dia de Santa Ana. The next day was *Santa Ana's* day. Every woman fortunate enough to own a riding horse and sidesaddle brought them out. And with a white sheet thrown over the saddle and tied underneath to keep the long flowing skirts from soiling, she rode off, dressed in all her finery, to join the other lady riders. When tired of riding, they dismounted at the dance, which continued through the hot afternoon into the night.

At big private dances, when the best musicians were

hired, the guitarist was usually a good singer and composer of improvised verses. Witty verses which he addressed to the dancers caused great merriment. This gift was evident, and lovely ballads as well as simpler songs were composed even by sheepherders.

I was now to lose the only playmate who lived near me. (Who would I invite now as *madrina* for my doll's baptisms and weddings? Lupe always made little cakes and spicy *mistela* for those little parties.) My cousin, Octavia, was going to be married. A month after the proposal and three days before the wedding, the groom, accompanied by his parents and sisters, arrived at the bride's home. Behind their carriage came a chef in a wagon loaded with provisions for the wedding feast and the big trunk with the bride's trousseau.

As soon as they arrived, the *prendorio* or announcement of the marriage took place, and the introduction of the couple to relatives and friends. Both families assembled in the parlor. The father presented the bride to the groom's father saying: "Here you have the jewel you are seeking." The groom's father took her by the arm and introduced her to his family. Then he introduced his son to the bride's family.

The big trunk with the trousseau next was brought in and presented to the bride. In it were the white satin gown, veil, wax flower wreath, the white shoes, gloves, set of combs, other silk gowns and set of jewels. Then the groom's relatives presented their gifts. Refreshments were served, and the house was placed at the disposal of the groom's family, who took charge of the wedding preparations. Invitations were distributed by messengers. The matron of honor and best man were invited.

While the cooks heated the adobe oven and baked the rolls, cookies and cakes and roasted the chickens, the men sprinkled, rolled, and packed the ground in the courtyard, preparing it for the dance. They hung lanterns on each porch post, decorated with evergreen branches. On one corner of the porch an altar was prepared by covering a table with lace curtains and decorating it with candles and flowers. Before this improvised altar the wedding took place at seven o'clock in the evening. My brother and I carried the bride's train. Behind us marched the matron of honor with the best man, parents and relatives. After the ceremony, the musicians, playing a march, led the guests to the long *sala*, where the dinner was served. Several times the long table was filled with guests. At the end of the dinner, the bridal couple led the grand march around the enclosed court. When the march turned into a round waltz, my brother, thinking we should still follow the bride, kept whirling me around so fast that I soon was so dizzy my head hung back limp. My mother caught sight of my undignified position and grasped brother by the arm, stopping his fun and the merriment the guests were having at my expense.

During the dance a few guests at a time were invited into the *sala* to partake of the refreshments that had been placed on the table after it was cleared of the dinner dishes.

The arrival of a new baby was always announced by word sent by a messenger saying: "Mr. and Mrs. so and so announce that you have another servant at your command." It was during the following summer that my cousin brought her new baby and came to visit her parents, and invited my parents to stand as godparents for her baby's christening. Mother dressed the baby in a long, starched, white linen dress trimmed with a lot of tucking and embroidery ruffles, to which the baby seemed to object, judging by the demonstration of temper he gave us.

When the family returned from the church after the baptism, mother handed the baby back to his mother with a little verse. Refreshments were then served to the invited guests.

Baby Felix must now be confirmed. It was during my school vacation. Pompous Archbishop Chapelle, accompanied by his secretary and the Taos parish priest, arrived at our house one evening for the purpose of administering confirmation the following morning in our private chapel. The archbishop was too particular to hold the services in the old church in the upper village. Our home, since my grandfather's time, had been the home for the prelates. I felt honored to give up my new bedroom for our distinguished guest.

CHAPTER VIII

In the Royal Village of the Holy Faith

By my fifth year at the Convent School in Taos, I noticed that I was making slow progress in my grades. No exams were held. There were no promotions, only the beginning of a higher reader, an Olendorf, or some other new book, added to the same grade. I told my father about it and preparations were made for my entrance at the Loretto Academy, at La Villa Real de La Santa Fe. Autumn's coloring brush had already touched the little valley turning its summer greenery into bright fall shades. Flocks of wild ducks flew overhead on their journey to the south. Meadowlarks sang their morning song, robins chirped on tree tops, and all nature smiled out of doors this bright sunny morning, as if trying to cheer my sad heart at parting with my loving family. My father and I started in our one-seated buggy on our two and a half days trip to La Villa. A stop for the first night's rest was made at Los Luceros, where my father's uncles, Don Nemecio and Lucas Lucero, lived in the big double house built by their father, Don Diego. The house stood on top of a high hill commanding a beautiful view of the Chama and Rio del Norte valleys.

This was the region of the explorer Oñate. Here with his courageous colonizers and pious friars, Oñate founded the first Spanish settlement and built the first church near San Juan de Los Caballeros, and started a culture of religion, arts, and science in the New Spain, even before the Atlantic seaboard was settled. The industries of weaving and wood carving started here. His craftsmen carried in their minds their patterns depicting a true artistic talent. The Spanish not being influenced by outside sources, preserved these arts better in New Mexico than in other countries. The first Spanish drama of *"Los Moros"* was given during the dedication of the church.

From Taos we traveled over the old road, *"El Camino Militar,"* which connected Fort Garland with Fort Marcy in Santa Fe.

By the end of our second day's ride we descended the Tesuque Hill just as the last rays of the fading sun painted in bloody hues the mighty Sangre de Cristo Range which rose majestically behind the towers of the Cathedral of Saint Francis. The cathedral bells' silvery notes chiming the *"Ave Maria"* floated through the air. We entered the plaza, steeped in evening peace and deserted except by a few men standing in front of dimly oil lamp-lit saloons. Oil lanterns set on posts on each corner of the park relieved the darkness at night.

My father's aunt, Mrs. Gaspar Ortiz, welcomed us to her home on the corner of Rio Chiquito, on the site of the present Montezuma Hotel. From a two-story building with white portals the house gradually sloped down into a one story building on the corner of San Francisco Street. In the large room on this corner was *"El Numero Cuatro,"* the only large grocery store in town.

I found this city of the Holy Faith rich in its three centuries of glamorous early history and still holding to many of the old Spanish customs which injected that ancient flavor found so interesting by the newcomer. In evidence around the plaza square were the squeaky *carretas* loaded with wood and pulled by burros. Herds of these meek burden bearers went around the streets loaded with wood, *amole* root and other vintages. The driver, a typical native, poked the donkeys with a stick to keep them moving. On the sunny Old Palace porch squatted old women beggars, stretching their

49

shaky hand to passersby for an alm. Church bells frequently were ringing the angelus, or tolling to mark the dawn and end of day. Black-shawled women and devout *caballeros* were seen hastening to church. High adobe walls enclosed attractive patios and orchards, and Rio Chiquito Street was lined with dingy-looking markets and curio stores. In Mondragon's workshop one found exquisite gold and silver filigree jewelry, worked as fine as cobwebs. Other pieces were copies of expensive gold sets adorned with precious stones.

All these antiques and customs charmed me then as they still do. The big, attractive, old-style homes were still well-kept, with their long, deep-walled, cool *salas de recibo,* and *placitas* surrounded with neat, whitewashed porches. One of these most attractive old homes was the home of Aunt Magdalena's sister, my Aunt Cleofas Garcia, on Alto Street. Another one was Don Felipe Delgado's home, on the corner of Burro Alley and San Francisco Street, where the Lensic Theater now stands. My cousin Lola took me on a visit to her Uncle Don Felipe's home. He was sitting reading in the *sala* when he saw us at the door. He quickly rose and came forward to meet us. A true type of the fine Spanish gentleman he was. His fair complexion was almost as white as his hair and his long white beard. All were accentuated by the spotless black Prince Albert suit he wore. The king of Spain had conferred on his father, Don Manuel Delgado, the rank of Captain of the Provincial Spanish New Mexico Army. Only a fine gentleman like him would trouble himself in entertaining a mere fifteen-year-old girl. He showed me his family photographs and then took us across the *placita,* surrounded by spotless white porches, to the garden. The charm of the city was enhanced by its hospitality.

As it was a two days' ride over a rough road from there to my home, I remained at school until it closed in the latter part of June. However, my aunt, Mrs. Ortiz, did not forget me, and on weekends during the Christmas and Easter vacations she would send my cousins, Carlota and Pita, to ask Sister to let me come to her home. Aunt Magdalena, of a humble exterior but known by all for her generous heart, exceeded anyone I have ever known, in hospitality. Her home was always filled with visiting relatives and friends. No matter how poor or humble the guest who came to her door, they always received the same hearty welcome, and room was made to accommodate them somewhere in an already full house. She was a Lucero, my grandfather's sister, and like all the Luceros, was the sweet, patient kind.

With a retinue of servants including cook, nurse, errand boy, seamstress and one or two other servants at their command, my aunt and her daughter, Cliefitas, had nothing else to do but to give orders and entertain company. Like all the Spanish ladies in her time, my aunt was very faithful in attending the church services every day, sometimes getting there so early, the church was not open. Once she was so wrapped up in prayers she did not hear the evening angelus bell, and when she went to leave the church she found herself locked in. She said she was not a bit worried and would have slept lying before the altar, but someone passing heard her knock and had the door opened. In the sanctuary is where she always found rest and peace from her bustling home. She had known and mentioned all the bishops and priests from the Mexican bishop, Zubirias, the famous Archbishop Lamy and the Vicar Egillon, to the then Acting Bishop Chapelle. Her husband, Don Gaspar, had been one of the most generous contributors to help Bishop Lamy build the cathedral of Saint Francis. He also donated the land from the river north for the opening of the street that bears his name, Gaspar Avenue.

Strange to say, the wife of such a wealthy man died poor and one of his daughters passed away in the old people's home. The daughter's husband had gambled away her wealth. All of Aunt Magdalena's sons were the leisurely kind of gentlemen, and when their wealth gave out they seemed to think that their mother's money was endless. They kept coming to her for help until her wealth gave out also, but she could never refuse them anything.

When I entered Loretto Academy, Sister Francis Lamy was the superior and Sister Mary Xavier was the academy prefect. In this school I found everything more modern and convenient. The buildings had electric light, steam heat and the great luxury of running water and bathrooms. The lovely gothic chapel was warm and comfortable and inspired faith and fervor with its beautiful statues. The boarders were friendly, and soon I felt myself perfectly at home. There was only one Spanish girl in my class, a descendant of the prominent Perea family; the rest were all Americans. Edith Saint Vrain, with her beautiful rosy complexion, dark eyes, and luxurious brown hair, was beautiful. Iren, her sister, was not pretty, but friendly. They were descendants of the early pioneer, Col. Ceran Saint Vrain.

Each year my studies became more interesting. There I could spread out into all the branches of study I could take. One day it occurred to me that I was neglecting my beloved language. I went to Sister Mary Xavier and I told her I would like to take some of my studies in Spanish. She looked at me quite amused. "And who is going to teach it to you?" she asked. I had not thought of that, but two days after, she told me that Sister Gertrude would give me Spanish grammar lessons twice a week after school. Rejoicing, I went to my lesson on the appointed days.

Every weekend we had to write to our parents. What should have been a pleasure became an irksome duty, for what news was there to tell? Nothing but the same thing happened week after week, and I was no composer. Church ceremonies were the chief distractions from our everyday routine. I was glad when a feast celebration came and I could describe it. Here at La Villa these were celebrated with more pomp and solemnity. The bishop officiated at the biggest functions. The Easter and Christmas masses were very impressive.

At my aunt's home on Christmas morning, boys came to the door calling *"mis Crismas."* Candy and other goodies given them were put into the flour bag they carried hanging on their backs.

The chief entertainment was the religious drama of *"Los Pastores."* This was acted very differently then from the way

IN THE ROYAL VILLAGE OF THE HOLY FAITH

I saw it performed a few years ago. I was disgusted at the way they now try to modernize this beautiful drama by dressing in pink sateen costumes, caps trimmed in glittering tinsel and the little pincushions pinned on their backs instead of the roll of blankets they used to have strapped there, the shabby clothes and water gourds hanging from their waist, and at the boisterous, laughing audience. They did not seem to feel the significance of the play as people used to. Even the children used to be quiet and respectful all during the performance.

During my third school year there, the Pallium was conferred on Bishop Chapelle by Cardinal Gibbons. Other high church dignitaries came to attend the solemn ceremony. At the end of over two hours of church service, the richly-garbed clergy marched with great pomp to Loretto hall, where a big banquet was held in honor of the great occasion. A semi-circle table was set at the head of the hall and from it ran two long tables on each side. Sister Xavier chose three of us senior girls to wait on the cardinal's table. Sister handed me the cardinal's plate, and when I set it down in front of him he stopped talking and asked me my name. I felt greatly flattered at this attention; however, I have learned since that great, prominent people are gracious and kind, even to little insignificant folks.

The cardinal's visit being the first by a prince of the church to the kingdom of Saint Francis was an occasion of great ecclesiastical pomp, and brought people from all over the state.

On visits at my aunt's home I heard many interesting stories. Political topics seemed to interest her guests. The story of the tragic death of Don Francisco Chavez filled me with horror. It had happened some years before, but it remained in the minds of the people. He had been so kind to his people, and was so well liked that he had been nick-named *"el padre de los pobres"* (the father of the poor). Don Francisco was such a strong Democrat that no matter which party was in power he always won his election until betrayed by one of his party and shot to death. As he fell on the bridge he said: *"Por detras soy sangre fria"* (From behind I am easy prey).

"Why don't you shoot?" asked one of the Borregos, coming up the bridge. "Don't you see that the man is dead?" answered one of the other men. Governor Thornton then appointed Cunningham to the sheriff's office and he brought several Texas Rangers to act as his deputies. After a lengthy investigation four suspects were arrested and charged with the crime.

Judge Laughlin, a Democrat, excused himself from presiding in the trial, and Judge Fall, a Republican, took his place, with Crist, a Democrat, as attorney for the Chavez family and Catron, a Republican, for the defense. Mr. Catron fought this case with great vigor carrying the case from court to court. The suit continued for years, ending at the Supreme Court, where the men were sentenced to the rope. This case brought great fame to Attorney Catron. Sometime before, he had, in some way, acquired ownership of the Tierra Amarilla Grant.

This grant of land had been deeded to my great grandfather, his eight sons and their heirs by the Spanish government. The deed contained a clause that no heir had a right to sell. The land was given to them to colonize or to use it as pasture or in any other way they needed. One of the heirs sold, it is said, only his share to Mr. Catron, but turned over to him the deed for the whole grant. Mr. Catron made a great profit by selling the whole grant to an Eastern company, and the many heirs each received a small amount. The first year I came to Santa Fe, modern, two-story brick houses were very rare. The Catron mansion on Grant and the Stabb one on Palace Avenue were such curiosities to us girls that we used to take walks just to see these homes with their nice green lawns and trees enclosed with wrought-iron fences instead of the high adobe walls, which selfishly hide the beauty of the grounds.

Friends going to the Corn Dance at the Santo Domingo Indian pueblo invited me to go with them. Just as the first

IN THE ROYAL VILLAGE OF THE HOLY FAITH

rays of the rising sun on the fourth of August spread over the valley, the population of the pueblo assembled on their housetops. They went through their Indian way of celebrating, pouring to their sun god, in soft voices, their prayers and songs. Later they assembled in the church to give praise to the white man's God and to the parish patron saint, Santo Domingo. The church services over, the Indian girls carried the statue of the saint and led the procession out of church, the drum man and weird flute, the gold-robed priest and faithful following. At the end of the street the girls placed the statue in a shrine built of standing logs. On the altar were several silk and bead bedecked wooden statues.

The crowd of white people took refuge from the hot sun under log shelters built against the houses. The Indians resumed their celebration ceremonies. At the end of the street appeared two lines of Koshares with two leaders in front. Their bodies were nude, faces and hair were whitewashed, and dark blue spots were painted all over them. A tuft of corn husks stuck up on top of their heads. All this was symbolic of spotted blue corn.

In perfect unison, with a prancing step, giving grunts, they advanced towards the shrine, paused, bowed every few steps. Repeating this, they continued until they stood in a last bow before the statues. From there they scattered, running in every direction, going into the houses and coming out again. Then followed a great sight. Out of the large kiva poured a stream of ornately costumed Indians, couple after couple, men coming up first. Then each couple descended the broad stairway. The last were a cute couple about eight years old.

Below stood a circle of Indian singers and drum men. Slowly the double line danced their way to the middle of the street. The spotted Koshares, representing clowns, appeared again, crossing back and forth between the dancers. There seemed to be no end to their monotonous dance, and the spectators who tired of watching went into the houses to buy some of the beautiful pottery on display. One can buy it in the pueblos much cheaper than in town.

ROMANCE OF A LITTLE VILLAGE GIRL

Another delightful little trip was to the feast of San Lorenzo at the pueblo of Picuris, near the village of Peñasco. The ride with our friends, the Whitlocks, through the Taos Canyon, was rough but scenic. The Indian village is situated up on the hills. It is now a small one, but must have been of some importance during the Spanish conquest. Castañeda in the history of Coronado's expedition mentioned it as having 2,000 population. Oñate is the first one to mention it in his entry, in 1598. Then Gen. De Vargas recorded his peaceful entry in 1692.

The small church, said to have been built in 1780, is picturesquely situated among the hills. After the feast day mass, the Indians had their customary dances, very much like the Taos Indian dances.

CHAPTER IX

An Invitation to a Wedding

The magic that wove an unexpected romance for the little village girl started at a wedding feast in the ancient village of Abiquiu. Cupid is never idle.

It was during my school summer vacation. My family received an invitation to a cousin's, Gonzales', wedding at Abiquiu. My father still clinging to the strict Spanish customs, gave my brother and me permission to go if mother would chaperone.

The fourteenth of August dawned bright and warm. Early breakfast finished, we hastened to depart on our all-day ride over the wide, rolling plain across the Rio Grande. In three hours we were walking down the steep, rock Petaca Hill; at the foot of the hill we climbed back into our buggy seat, rode past the village, basking in sunny desolation, and a few miles up entered the green valley of El Vallecito. The little adobe houses slept peacefully between the green farms strewn along the rich trout stream. Above rose the high mountain ridges. By hard pulls, our puffing tired team pulled up the last rise on the steep road, and at last, by sunset, we stood on the crest of the divide, with the El Rito valley lying green at our feet, drenched and sparkling with raindrops from a cloudburst that had just passed before us. Scenting the cool, fresh air our panting horses were refreshed and trotted in a lively manner down the mountain, splash-

57

ing golden raindrops from pools that reflected the rays of
the fast sinking sun. At the foot of the hill my brother drew
rein before the roaring stream. No bridge in sight, our buggy
plunged into the rushing water. Roughly shaking, tumbling
over the rocky river bed, we reached the other side and ascended the slight elevation upon which the Jaramillos' residence stood in a long zigzag of eighteen rooms. Two young
men had just stepped out of the front gate and started to
walk up the street. Hearing the noise of our carriage wheels,
they stopped and waited until our team came to a standstill
before them.

Venceslao Jaramillo recognized my brother and stepped
up to the buggy to shake hands. He invited us to come in.
My mother thanked him and said we were going up to her
Cousin Cleofita's house. "You will not be able to make the
crossing. The river is much deeper up there. You better stop
here, and by tomorrow the flood will be down," Cousin Ven
said. Following his advice we alighted from our buggy and
were introduced to our cousin, Tom Burns. We walked
through the long front porch and were met at the *saguan*
door by the hostess, Doña Ana Maria. Her two sisters, Doña
Piedad and Doña Josifita Burns, with their daughters, already had arrived on the way to the wedding.

That night the group of girls in the party were allotted
the south guest wing of the house for our quarters. The
family occupied the middle wing. In the back wing were the
office, servants' room with their kitchen, dining room and
store rooms. The guest wing was divided into two bedrooms
and parlor by blue plush and yellow satin-lined curtains
that hung from the ceiling to · drag on the cream-and-blue
flowered velvet carpet. Then followed the guests' dining
room, kitchen and living room. A low fire in the grey marble
fireplace in the parlor broke the chill from the dampness of
the rain storm.

It was a gay crowd that gathered at the breakfast table
next morning, all eager to start on our trip to Abiquiu.
However, Grandma Melita reminded us that it was the feast
of the Assumption and we must attend mass before leaving.

AN INVITATION TO A WEDDING

This postponed the ride until after lunch. Don Jesus Maria Jaramillo then arrived in his fine coach, a present from his father-in-law, Don Gaspar, to his daughter, Aunt Cleofitas. Cousins Pita and Carlota, his two daughters, were with him. The four carriages finally got started. We older girls crowded into the front carriage, with my brother driving. As we were nearing the village of Abiquiu we crossed a deep arroyo just ahead of a crest of rushing water coming down from a heavy rain up on the hills. We all jumped down to watch the other buggies make the crossing, as the flood had already reached it. With hard pulls encouraged by loud "gid-ups," the horses pulled the carriages out of the muddy water. Whooping "hurrahs" and scraping the mud off our shoes, we climbed back into our seats. Around the curve in the hills we came in sight of the fifteen-room mansion of Don Reyes Gonzales, a spacious, finely-furnished house, built for the gracious living of a Spanish Don's family, with Indian servants to serve them.

My mother, noticing on our arrival that Don Reyes' home was already filled with guests, decided to go across to the pueblo to stop at the home of Don Jose Maria Chavez, one of my fathers' cousins. One of the servants was sent on horseback to try the crossing of the flooding treacherous Chama River. With the high water almost rushing into our buggy, we crossed safely, climbed the hill to the small mesa and stood before an antique New Mexico-style house. The front *saguan* was closed by one of those rare, double high doors that had a small door cut out in one of the leaves of the larger one. These doors were built for safety against attacks of the Indians. The large door was kept closed and only the small one used. Although there was not such danger now, the custom was still adhered to for privacy. In answer to our knock the maid opened the small door. Bent almost in half we stepped over the high threshold to get in. Inside the hall we were met with a warm embrace by Cousin Jose Maria, a lively, versatile person. He ushered us into a lovely, red-carpeted parlor furnished in a black horsehair upholstered walnut suit. While he went out to call his wife I had time to notice the beautiful oil lamp hanging over the marble-top center table. The long lace curtains hanging from a fancy brass curtain rod were tied back with tasseled cords. Passing by the old kitchen, used now as a store room, I discovered an interesting type of a fireplace built in the corner with a *tapanco,* or shelf, over it, where dishes were kept before cupboards were known. We were being ushered to the dining room, across a cobblestoned courtyard. A rustic well, from which ice cold water was drawn, stood in the center.

Next morning Don Jose Maria took us through the side hall into the walled-in garden. From there we had a fine view of the sunlit, colored hills sheltering the green valley. Caves in the hills furnish white gypsum and red almangre for wall decorations, and the villages, La Plaza Blanca and La Plaza Colorado, take their names from the color of each hill beside them. From another cave *tequesquite* was out. This ingredient was used instead of baking powder for making the delicious Spanish cookies of the recipe that takes twenty-five egg yolks.

Abiquiu was first named by the Indians "Abechin," meaning hooting of an owl. The Spanish town was founded in 1747 but abandoned several times on account of the attacks of the Indians. With Spanish integrity, it was permanently resettled in 1770 by order of the Mexican viceroy. The Indians finally abandoned their village. The few who remained were taken as slaves by the Spaniards and gradually merged with the Spanish servants.

The ringing of the bell for the wedding mass cut short our pleasant stroll through the garden. We hastened in to don our hats.

At the church door, Cousin Jose Maria called our attention to the massive construction of the walls. "Look at these five-foot thick walls and lofty, carved ceiling. These are a monument to our forefathers who built them. I am opposed to having them torn down," he told us. Yet as soon as Don Jose Maria passed away, this great monument, which had patiently stood the storms of centuries, blending its contour so well with the landscape around it — like a page torn out of the book of the past — was replaced by a new church. This shows how little the new French priests appreciated the great faith our ancestors who labored to build these great shrines to the honor of God.

Guests and wedding party all assembled in the church. Our group of young girls took charge of the choir. Cousin Marguerite pumped hard on the rickety, dusty old organ to bring out a few faint tones.

The wedding mass over, we girls packed back into our buggy, giggling merrily, and followed the noisy wagon carrying the fiddlers playing a march on the way to *La Puente,* the bride's home. Introductions, reception and elaborate dinner followed, with the old days' formality and social importance observed then on these occasions.

By two o'clock in the afternoon the young people began getting restless for something to do. "Isn't there a place where we can dance?" asked Cousin Ven. "Yes, there is the old sala," answered Marcelino, the bride's brother. The double doors of the old sala were opened. Two of the men servants swept it and carried in seats. The musicians were called in and a gay dance started. In those days of smooth waltzes and swinging quadrilles, dancing was the joy of youth. Some of the older folks danced the graceful old *varsovianas* and *cunas.* This was before jazz music turned us into tap dancers.

The news of the dance spread in the village, and the door was packed with standing men. We began smothering with the heat. The groom sent two men up on the roof and they swept the earth from two squares, one at each end, lifted the cedar rajas sticks and — oh, joy! — the fresh air poured down on our heads. Refreshed, we kept on dancing until we were called in to supper. Later we went back to resume the dancing.

Dawn was lightening the eastern sky when the dance ended and the bridal party, relatives and friends went into the parlor to witness the *entriega.*

Cousin Tom, who had not left my side all during the dance — borrowing his sister's big black fan to cool me off

61

after each dance — still stood by my side, asking me to explain what was going on. This was a difficult task, to translate the long string of impromptu verses that the guitarist was addressing to the newlyweds, their parents and *padrinos* (attendants), verses of advice, of parting and blessings. At the end of this ceremony, hot coffee and rolls were served to the remaining guests, and each party left for their different lodgings to take a rest.

I felt too exhausted and excited to sleep. I got up and went into the parlor to look at the photographs in the blue velvet album. My heart gladdened. Here was Cousin Ven's picture. He had been all attention to me, inviting me out for almost every dance. He had attracted me from the very first time I met him. In the midst of my reverie my brother called at the door: "Come, we are ready to leave." By night we were back at El Rito, and left early the next morning for our home.

CHAPTER X

Back at Boarding School

Three weeks after, back at boarding school, a mail package was handed to me. I tore it open and found in it a high-buttoned shoe that I had forgotten under my bed at El Rito. But who sent it? A very small "V. J." on the left corner of the wrapping paper answered me. A few days later, another mysterious package came. I went into a corner in the recreation hall to open it. It was the mate to my other shoe, with a red, white and blue ribbon laced through the button holes and a bow at the top with a card pinned to it, saying: "Please acknowledge receipt. T. D. B." I rushed upstairs to my desk, brought out my dictionary and looked for the long word "acknowledge" and found "to confess, to avow." Hm, smart, trying to start a correspondence? I shall not write first, I mused.

On the first of November I was called to the prefect's office. What offense had I committed, I asked myself as I walked along the long corridor. In answer to my timid knock on the door and Sister Xavier's "Come in," I walked to her desk and stood behind her chair. "What is this Venceslao Jaramillo to you?" she asked, picking up a dainty little package from her desk. "My cousin," I answered. "Nothing more?" she asked. "Nothing more," I answered, for although very much impressed by this young man, I had not as yet thought of him in any other light. "As long as he is so honest, take this and say nothing to the girls, for we do not allow girls to receive presents from boys," she said. With burning face I took the package to my room and raised the top of my desk while I opened it so no one would see me. It was a lovely pearl pin, twisted with a gold thread, gold knob and band, and my initials engraved on it. "Happy birthday, V. J." was written on a card. The smarty, how had he found out it was my birthday?

Two months later, one morning at recess time, my Cousin Carlota came up to me saying: "Cousin Ven is here in the legislature. He will be passing by here to the college, where the legislature is meeting." Up to the sodality chapel I ran after lunch to watch the groups of legislature men pass. At last there came the young man with the familiar graceful swing to his step. He was wearing a brown Stetson hat and brown coat with a brown beaver fur collar. Puffing a cigarette, he was in an animated conversation with the two members who accompanied him. Yes, this was my Romeo — and that was the way I had begun to think of him, now that I had found out he was interested in me.

The capitol building had burned down. The fire was believed to have been started by an incendiary. Building a new one had to wait until the legislature voted an appropriation. So the legislature meetings were held at the St. Michael's College. When the house of representatives convened, the Democrats found that they lacked three members of having a majority. They succeeded in unseating two Republicans and then, finding out that young Jaramillo was not quite twenty-one years old, a fight started to unseat him. His friends, Capt. Max Luna and Mayor Lewyllen (members of the famous Rough Riders first volunteer regiment of the Spanish-American War) and Charles Spiess (the San Miguel County "Black Eagle") rose to his help. They made long, eloquent speeches in his favor. In the meantime, the young man's twenty-first birthday arrived and saved the situation.

"Sister Xavier wants you at the office," one of the nuns said to me. "Legislature time is a good time to have an entertainment," Sister Xavier said as I entered her office, "and

BACK AT BOARDING SCHOOL

I want you to pantomine 'I Stood at the Bridge at Midnight,' written by Longfellow." I felt flattered, and every day I went through the practice with her with great interest.

Girls were fluttering here and there in flounced gowns and puffed curls, chatting merrily. One of them brought me a long narrow box. "Help me open it, quick," I said, tearing the box open, capturing breathlessly a perfume that lingered insistantly in my memory. Rose and cream roses lay buried in a bed of green moss. Who had guessed so well what I was wearing? The roses matched exactly the rose-colored dress trimmed in cream brocaded silk and cream lace that I had chosen.

Sister Xavier's "Come" reach my ears from the stage door. In a hurry I pinned a rose of each color on my left shoulder and stepped up on the bridge built by the stage door. Behind me dropped a black curtain with a church steeple, and shiny stars scattered here and there. Sister Xavier's full, vibrating voice rose behind the curtain. "I stood at the bridge at midnight" echoed through the hall. As in a dream I went through the motions of my pantomine. A loud applause rose from the audience. I glanced over the sea of heads and the glitter of a pair of gold opera glasses caught my eyes at the foot of the stage. I bowed again to hide the hot flush that suffused my face. The curtain dropped down, and I was out bustling among my roses to find the card. Here it was, "With best wishes, Ven." I grabbed the box, ran up to the sodality chapel, placed the roses in a vase, set it at the foot of the white statue of Mary and knelt before it: "Bless my Romeo," came the whisper from my heart and lips.

This young man had begun to fill my mind, for each day I found in him more, his abilities, his social popularity and strong character. His polished manners and friendliness were growing into my heart. I was not the only one attracted by his friendly personality. Governor Otero had become one of his best friends and conferred on him the rank of colonel on his aide-de-camp staff, and he proved to be the youngest

65

colonel in the United States. He attracted me more now in the rich blue and gold-trimmed uniform. Governor Otero required great military pomp, and his military staff was richly uniformed.

The day after the entertainment being a Saturday, my cousins, Pita and Carlota, called for me to take me to their home. On the way I stopped at the photographers and had my picture taken wearing a spray of my precious roses, the first beautiful hothouse roses I had ever seen. That afternoon while we girls were sitting, playing a card game of *Porazo,* Ven came in and handed us tickets he had bought us and my aunt for "The Bohemian Girl." Lacking an opera house, the play was held at the courthouse. We arrived early and were amused to see through the black curtain the actors on the stage still applying last touches of their make-up. I tried to call Ven's attention to it, but his eyes were fastened on three persons just coming in. "Here comes my friend Max, his wife, and their guest, Miss Trini. Yesterday they took me to meet her at the station and invited me to come with them tonight," he said. As the three passed us, their glance traveled from Ven to me. They gave me a freezing look, but I never suspected why. A year after I was married, a friend told me the story. Miss Trini was engaged to marry Max, and a few weeks before the wedding she invited her friend (the present Mrs. Max) to come to visit her and be her bridesmaid. During the visit the friend and the fiance fell in love with each other and got married. Trini had been so sweet and forgiving that, feeling remorse, Mrs. Max since she met Ven, thought he would make an ideal husband for Trini. She thought she would be doing something to make it up to her friend for stealing her groom if they could interest Ven to marry her. She invited Trini to come to Santa Fe to visit her and tried her best to make a match, but their efforts failed.

The rest of the school days went by slowly, but everything has its end. Five months later I found myself reunited with my big, happy family of brothers and a new baby sister, who had taken the privilege of increasing the number of members in the family during my absence. She was already at the cute age of eight months, and I was delighted at having a sister.

"Some mail for you," my father said, handing me a letter at the supper table. Noticing the "V. J." on the corner of the linen envelope, I retired to my room to read the letter. A very formal note it was: "Dear Miss C. I have received your father's permission to correspond with you and hope that your missives will come often, telling me all you do, which will be of great interest to me. Ven." I lost my appetite for my supper and sat dreaming, pressing the letter to my heart. This genteel young man had become my ideal suitor and had changed my mind from my becoming a nun or remaining an old spinster.

The square, heavy linen envelope came in the mail regularly in every two weeks. In August a letter read: "I have bought a fine phaeton and team of higly-spirited horses and I am enjoying breaking them in, for mother and I are contemplating taking a trip to Arroyo Hondo in the very near future, to ask your parents for your hand in marriage." The nerve of this young man, I thought; I still have another year to finish my high school.

But every evening I stood at the front porch gate straining my eyes over the broad plain across the Rio Grande, in hopes of seeing a black speck or cloud of dust on the road.

Disappointed, I had given up my watch when, one evening, one of my brothers came running into my room saying: "Brother says there comes Jaramillo crossing the river in a phaeton." Did everyone know my secret? Mother flung off her white apron and walked out to meet the guests. I stood timidly inside the parlor door, half hiding, and stepped forward to shake hands very seriously as the guests came in the door.

The family all gathered in the parlor after supper. During a pause in the conversation, Dona Ana Maria moved uneasily in her chair, stood up with a proud swish of the rustling train on her black silk skirt, and very formally addressed my parents: "The object of our visit here is to ask for your daughter, Miss C., in marriage with my son, V." My father stood up and answered: "We will consider the proposal and give the answer in due time." A long pause followed during which my face became hotter and hotter. My baby sister, toddling in, broke the embarrassing silence. Mother's sister hearing about the proposal said to mother, "My brother-in-law was getting ready to come and propose to Cleofitas." Mother just to tease me would say: "*Pobrecitas de las feas si no hubiera malos gustos.*" This proverb translated means that if there weren't men with bad taste the poor ugly ones would never be proposed to. I, not being so fair and blue-eyed as some of my brothers and cousins, was considered the ugly, thin, pale duckling. But this never worried me; as the only girl, I was a favorite anyway.

That summer my parents were more than usually indulgent with me. Mother took me to a big wedding at Taos in July. In September, Mr. Asinger came to take orders for our store and invited my father to go for the Albuquerque fair, saying he would reserve a room for him. My father at this most busy season of the year could not absent himself, and sent my brother with me. Brother found a room at the old Franciscan Hotel. Next morning, while sitting in the hotel parlor, I was pleasantly surprised to see Ven walking in, looking very handsome in full colonel's uniform. He sat across the bay window from me, chatting. In came Governor Otero, to call him and tell him that the parade was getting ready to start. Seeing some ladies step out into the balcony, I followed them. Down on the street in front were the governor's mounted aides-de-camp, three colonels and captain all in full uniform. My Romeo, looking up at me with a broad smile, lifted his plumed cap in salute. My face flushed with pride and happiness as the ladies on the balcony turned and gave me a searching look.

Later in October, my father took me with him to join a party of his friends at Taos who were going to the Silver Serpent carnival in Denver. On arriving in Denver the first thing Mr. Leibert and my father did was to take Miss Leibert and me to the Daniels & Fisher store to do some shopping. She being older and wiser, bought a nice tailored suit. I, as usual, careful about spending money, looked for something not expensive but unusual. I bought a black silk neck boa and a pretty, crinkled silk waist front shaded from very pale green at the collar down to very dark green at the waist. At one o'clock the parade of beautiful floats passed down Broadway Street. That evening the carnival queen presided at the Silver Serpent dance, held in an enclosure on Broadway.

Another invitation was received, to the wedding of the other Gonzales cousin at San Luis, Colorado. One of my uncles and his wife invited my brother and me to go with them. In a hurry we fixed my green dress with the pretty green front bought in Denver, and I wore it with my green velvet bolero and brown chenille hat, which was trimmed with a pretty green feather. In San Luis we stopped at Don Antonio Baca's home. Charming Mrs. Baca still preserved the rosy bloom on her cheeks at eighty years. Was fate following me? Next morning when we took our seat in the church for the wedding, who did I see in the seat in front of us but Ven Jaramillo and his family. Perhaps they thought I knew they were to be there and had planned to attend. The wedding was in the accustomed simple country style. After the church ceremony a reception with refreshments was held at the bride's home. At noon the dinner was served, and the reception continued in the afternoon. After supper the dance started early at the courthouse hall and lasted until about midnight. Odila Salazar was truly a beautiful bride. Her pale blue satin gown accentuated her alabaster white complexion, vivid rosy cheeks and black eyes. I was happy to have met this lovely family of five girls and two boys and their fine parents.

My last school year my mother decided to spend the cold winter months in Santa Fe, and I stayed with her until the month of March, when she went home and I went in as a boarder again at Loretto. I had to give up my vehicle. Mother had allowed me to buy a very nice one, for I was not staying behind on any new fad my girl friends had.

I continued my music and the business course I had started, although not dreaming that I would ever make use of it. I took it merely because I wanted to learn all that I saw the other girls learning.

My Romeo did not forget me. At every feast day an appropriate gift came. At Christmas I had received a lovely green plush box with a complete ivory toilet set. For Valentine, a beautiful light blue silk and celluloid guitar-shaped valentine, with pink roses and forget-me-nots hand painted around the base, gilt strings held with ivory screws, and wide blue ribbon bow and streamers to hang it up. I was delighted, but I must hide it in my clothes closet before any of the girls saw it. Sister Xavier was the only one, I thought, who knew my secret, as the packages came by mail.

Towards the last of June, on commencement day, our classes stood on the stage to have gold medals pinned on our breasts and white flower wreaths placed on our heads by the archbishop.

My mother had come to take me home and was stopping at my aunt's home. Ven was in town and had left at my aunt's for me a box of large red roses. Flowers tell an age-old language of tender thoughts.

Next day, a Sunday, he came with a driver in a two-seated surrey and invited the family for a ride around the plaza. We parked to hear the band concert given by fat Don Pacho's well-trained musicians. I had pinned on my dress a couple of the red roses, not dreaming the attraction and comments these would cause among my acquaintances in the park. "What do red roses mean?" they were asking my girl chum, Nora. "Love, of course," was the answer. This went into my autograph album in which my dear schoolmates had written endearing little verses before parting. I kept the album many years after to remind me of my happy school days.

BACK AT BOARDING SCHOOL

A few days' rest were given our team after our return from Santa Fe before my father departed on a mysterious trip. No one seemed to know he had gone except my brother, who whispered to me, "He has gone to El Rito." What kind of answer had he taken? I had not been consulted.

The dainty little box that came in the next mail left me without doubt. By the size of the package I guessed what it must contain; so I waited until I was alone in my room to open it.

Before going to bed I lit the oil lamp on my marble top table, and stood holding my left hand under its shade, admiring the bright sparkle of the big diamond solitaire on my third finger. "It's precious and tempting, but — " I turned the light out and stood at the window, leaning my elbows on the sill, gazing at the moon rising over the *capilla* tower across the garden. I pondered for a while. Funny way of becoming engaged — through the mail. Why didn't he have the courage to give me the ring when he saw me in Santa Fe? It shall go back, I decided, moving back to the table. I lit the lamp, wrote on a little card, "Too big," placed the card with the ring in the box and addressed it.

My brother was canceling the stamps on the mail that was to leave next morning. "Mail this, please," I said, setting the little package on the desk. He must have told my mother about it, for the following night mother came into my room and said: "Do as you like but you will never find another boy like Venceslao." I was so shy that at the mere mention of his name my color mounted to a deep pink and I did not answer a word. My mother left the room and I threw myself sobbing on my bed. Yes, she was right, but why didn't I explain that my struggle was choosing between her and my Romeo? I wanted to spend at least another year with her, and even wanted a year at one of those fine colleges I saw advertised in my *Home Journal* magazine. Then those relatives of his would not be bragging to me about their fine Notre Dame school they had attended one year.

The next letter received from Ven was a sad one, saying, "I have returned the ring to Spitz to have it made smaller

71

and trust that you will accept it then. If you refuse, I will never want another woman to cross my path." If he would only keep that promise, I would keep him waiting another year; but there were too many nice girls after him and my impatient Romeo might get tired of waiting and marry one of them. That would kill me, I thought. When the ring came back, I kept it.

CHAPTER XI

School Dreams Blossom into a Wedding

The following week's mail brought me a cheerful letter: "Be prepared to go to Denver with mother and me to buy your trousseau." (It is a Spanish custom for the bridegroom to buy the trousseau and pay all the wedding expenses.)

He brought with him his mother and two sisters. On our way to Denver, a day's stop at the Antlers Hotel in Colorado Springs was a delightful visit for our party. The terraces and park opening from the hotel lobby were a restful place to sit and enjoy the view of the grand scenery. The scenic splendor and magnificence of the 14,100-foot high Pikes Peak mountain, covered with snow in midsummer, is a marvelous sight. At the Garden of the Gods we had our pictures taken on burros, before the Balancing Rock. In the evening we attended the band concert in the park at the entrance of Cheyenne Canyon and drove in to see the beautiful waterfalls.

Reaching Denver, our party stopped at the Brown Palace Hotel. I had never been in such a grand hotel before, but by my outer reserve no one would have known that I had not been accustomed all my life to having French waiters placing footstools under my feet and setting silver platters before me. At the Daniels & Fisher Store, where my trousseau was made by Madame Belcher, she stood me on a platform for hours every day, pinning and unpinning lace and

73

chiffon frills on wedding and dinner gowns, draping on the illusion veil, a short length to fall over my face, the other end to drop at the back for the length of my gown. The wedding gown was of duchess white satin, veiled in embroidered silk grenadine, trimmed with myriads of chiffon frills and pearl passementerie. Between the taffeta lining was a soft padding, then another ruffled taffeta drop-skirt. I could hardly carry the weight of the long train. The traveling tailored suit was of brown broadcloth, and I bought a green figured blouse and a straw sailor hat, trimmed with a Roman striped ribbon sash, to go with it. "She is the tiniest bride I have ever seen," the madame would say to her helper, making me feel like a very small, insignificant being, and wondering how Ven had ever picked me out.

The trousseau at last finished, we left for El Pueblo, where we stopped to ask Mr. Hinkle, a friend, to send us a good chef to prepare the wedding feast. At a crockery store we ordered five complete dinner sets and some crystal vases, two for each table. At a bakery, the clerk asked us what kind of wedding cake we wanted. "We make a white and a fruit cake, three-tier ones, for twenty-five dollars each," he said. "Send us one of each kind," Ven told him. At the jewelry store, Ven bought five silver table sets. My mother-in-law, seeing a four-piece tea set, said she wanted to get me one with my name engraved. "You want this name on the four sets?" the clerk asked. "Yes," Ven answered. On the four pieces, I timidly corrected, but I was not heard, and the four sets, on four round silver platters, came with my name and wedding date engraved on each. By now I was bewildered and said: "How extravagant!" "Oh, well, I intend to be married just once," Ven said. For the flowers and wedding bouquet, Rousenwal was sending the order in; so we left for my home.

I want a quiet wedding in the *capilla,* I told the family. Ven answered, "That will never do. The last time I was in Santa Fe I met Governor Otero and he said, Colonel, I and my staff are coming to your wedding. We can not accommodate all those people here. Tomorrow we go to Taos and arrange for rooms at the hotel." The following morning when we left for Taos the few flitting white clouds on the clear blue sky gave no indication of the impending storm; but before we were halfway, there wasn't a speck of blue sky to be seen. The strongest downpour descended on us. Flash after flash of vivid lightning lit the dark sky. At every reverberating peal of thunder, Ven's team would jump and try to get away, but Ven with set lips held tight to the reins. By the time we reached the Arroyo Seco Hill the storm had abated; it passed as quickly as it came. At a small house by the road we stopped to ask the man standing at the door if he would try the river crossing below on his horse. He shook his head "no." I went into the house while Ven went down to take a look at the crossing. The man said to his wife in Spanish: "Let that gringito get into that swift water and we will see him with his legs up in the air." I did not let on that I had heard him. When Ven returned I told him what the man had said. We had better turn home and come back tomorrow, I said.

Next day a perfect July day arched the blue heavens. I again sat by my Romeo in timid silence. The only indication I ever had of his great affection for me during his courtship was a warm, smiling look, to which I answered in the same way. If he had attempted to show his love by petting, like they do now, I would have lost my respect for him and refused to marry him. I had agreed to marry him because I had found in him my ideal of a perfect gentleman, always respectful.

We reached Taos in time to attend mass at Guadalupe church. Then we went to see Father Pouget, the rector, to make arrangements for the marriage ceremony, and from there went to the Hotel Barron and rented the dance hall, five bedrooms, a sitting room and kitchen.

Mr. Albert Muller had seen us arrive on the plaza and came to invite us to have lunch at his home. His wife was very charming, as was he and his beautiful eight-year-old-daughter whom I invited to be one of my little flower girls.

The other one was Amelia Barron. Both had a bewitching mass of black, long curls and black eyes.

The Jaramillos left next day for El Rito to return in a week for the wedding.

A very busy week followed. I had been studying about the Denver weddings in the *Post* that my brother received, and now I wrote notes to four young girls at Taos asking them to be my bridesmaids. Ven had already asked Mr. and Mrs. T. D. Burns to stand with us, as best man and matron of honor. I ordered linen suits, tan shoes and white straw sailor hats for my four younger brothers, and a pink silk dress for baby sister. The family all outfitted, two days before the big affair found us and the Jarmillos again in Taos, putting on the final touches to the wedding preparations. We went to the Muller store and rented more dishes. I bought four little gold stickpins to give my bridesmaids as favors. The chef with a wagon full of boxes of food for the feast, and Rousenwal, with another load of boxes with the fresh flowers and other ornaments for the dining hall decorations, had arrived. Even a new canvas ceiling had to be put on in the hall. So there was an army of helpers, with everybody rushing here and there. My trousseau and bouquet of white roses and dainty bell lilies got there — I don't know how. Ven's gifts to me were a crescent diamond pin, a gold watch with a diamond star in the center and long gold chain, and three little pearl and diamond pins with which to pin my veil. He had thought of everything.

CHAPTER XII

Wedding at Taos

In 1898, the year of my wedding, the town and its surrounding villages scattered throughout the beautiful Taos valley were still but little changed from the time Don Juan de Oñate established the first capital of New Spain there. The old mission church which always impressed me with its sacredness in its silent, simple but massive strength, was still standing. For centuries the rain had washed down so many layers of mud plaster that the earth had formed mounds all around the edifice, making it appear a part of the earth elevation on which it stood.

The old town was now preparing to receive one of Governor Bent's successors, Governor Miguel Antonio Otero. The businessmen were hanging flags around the plaza and showing great enthusiasm in giving the governor a warm reception, as he was always given on his visits to the different towns. He was the most popular governor.

During his nine years of able and concientious administration as chief executive he brought the territory to financial and progressive advancement. His influence reached even to the White House during the administration of President William McKinley, by whom he was appointed chief executive of the territory. He was a man of diminutive stature, big in mind and energy.

He and his party were to arrive in Taos the evening before our wedding day. Guests were arriving from different towns in Colorado and New Mexico.

The plaza square was crowded with a throng of people, eager to see the governor. Seven, eight and nine o'clock —fireworks were booming, flags were waving — but no governor arrived. The crowds, tired of waiting, finally dispersed.

Next morning by ten o'clock the governor, his wife, their two young lady guests, Cols. Hersey and Austin and their wives, the orchestra from Santa Fe, and the T. D. Burns family arrived, Mrs. Burns wearing black. Their nephew, Tom Sargent, had been killed by lightning on his way home to El Rito in that terrific electric storm that Ven and I had met on our way to Taos.

A train wreck on a washout near Espanola had caused the delay in the governor's arrival. The priest who was on his way to help the Taos priest was injured in the wreck and had been taken back to the hospital in Santa Fe, where he died. Had I been supersititious I might have taken these incidents as a bad omen, but my heart was too full of unsullied bliss to have room for gloomy foreboding.

The Taos residents were certainly proving their hospitality. Dr. Martin, Lord Mamby, the Leiberts and others offered to help house our guests, and the governor's party, the Burns', and many others found comfortable lodging in these attractive homes. Some of the invited guests called that morning to meet the bridal couple. One woman exclaimed when we were introduced; *"Oh, que novios tan esquisitos!"* (What an exquisite bridal couple!) Would people ever let me forget my diminutive size?

> In memory's reliquary I stored away
> This red-letter day;
> With no apprehension of the scars
> That later painful events would leave.

Preparations were all complete. The dining hall was a bower of festoons of green smilax and fresh flowers. The walls were covered with greens and hoops covered with fresh flowers. At the head of the hall, on a platform, stood a double wrought-iron arch with feathery ferns trailing over it. In the center hung a large bell covered with moss and flowers, and under it were placed seats for the bridal party. At the other end was a balcony for the orchestra.

Five long tables ran the width of the hall, decorated with flowers and with the wedding cakes on the two center ones.

At the appointed hour of seven o'clock in the evening, the spacious church filled to capacity with guests in festive array.

I sent Ven and the best man, Mr. Burns, ahead to wait for us at the church, and rode in a carriage with Mrs. Burns, the matron of honor, and my father. We were followed by the four bridesmaids in another carriage. When Ven's uncle saw me walking into the church on my father's arm, he looked around for the bridegroom and not finding him, frantically rushed into the church and called him out (the Spanish custom was for the bride to walk in with the bridegroom). To my embarrassment here came Ven and Mr. Burns to meet us halfway down the church aisle. I frowned, whispering, "Why did you come out?" With a broad smile the two fell in line behind us. Not having time to think that the giving away could have taken place right there, we walked up to the altar that way. We had attended the six o'clock mass at the convent chapel that morning, so now it was just the marriage ceremony.

The simple ceremony over, I took Ven's arm and he started walking down the aisle in a hurried lively step. I squeezed his arm, whispering "March slowly."

The two long parlors at the Barron Hotel filled up with the guests. Congratulations ended, we marched in to the dinner. Rousenwal, in change of the decorations, had not figured that when the chairs were pulled out there would not be room for the waiters to pass between the tables, so only one side of each table was used, and part of the guests had to wait for a second table. With only one chef, and two inexperienced women to help him in the kitchen, the food was served in platters to be passed around the tables by the boy waiters, also with little experience. After the meat course here they came with the ice cream and coffee. Where was the delicious chicken salad the chef had prepared from fat chickens he had brought all the way from Pueblo? A large dishpan full was thrown away next morning, spoiled. The salad plates were there, but the women did not know. They wanted to serve it in platters like the other food, and the platters were all used. One of my cousins thinking they should be serving something to go with the meat course asked one of the waiters: "Isn't there some fruit?" The boy rushed to the kitchen and came with a handful of oranges which he dropped by her plate. (It was a good thing I did not see this.) Wine cups, we had forgotten to order, and the fine, sparkling Cresta Blanca wines were not served. The beautiful wedding cakes sat on the center of the table untouched, forgotten. Ven sat chatting with the governor, seated at his side, perfectly unaware of my worried look, which Mrs. Otero caught once and answered with a sweet, reassuring smile.

When the waiters announced there were second tables to be served, the chef gave up, tore his apron off and went to his room. The waiters and the women did their best, but I was afraid to ask what the second tables had been served. The young men, anxious to start dancing, began bundling the tablecloths with silver and all and throwing them into the pantry before some of the last guests had left the tables.

One of my uncles came in and whispered something to Ven, and he got up and left the room. When Ven reached the dining room some of the tables were going out the back door into the yard. Indians were coming up the cellar door with bundles of wine bottles in their blankets, carrying them out to the drivers, already half drunk on their buggy seats out in the backyard.

The dance lasted until late. Next morning before the governor's party and relatives left I cut the white wedding cake. Ven had sent some bottles of wine to their rooms. What became of the fruit cake I never knew until told recently by a friend who attended the wedding that Ven had cut it and had it passed to the second tables. The reception which the

WEDDING AT TAOS

Taos business men had arranged to give the governor the following night was given in our honor, as the governor already had left. One of our guests, Senator Barela, for many years in the Colorado senate from Las Animas County, was asked to give a speech. He gave a very complimentary talk about my husband, to which Ven responded in equally highly complimentary terms about the senator's very influential career. Swelled with pride at my smart husband, I sat by the senator's wife and other guests who had remained to attend the reception and dance.

The following day the family and relatives went to Arroyo Hondo, and on the next morning we left on our wedding trip to California. "What a mess of a wedding we had," I said to Ven, once we found ourselves in the Pullman car. "Forget it. Everybody had a good time," he replied. I should not have said this. He worked so hard to have everything so nice. He had seen that everything got there on time — chef, feast, dishes, trousseau, decorator, orchestra and even the guests. Every day teams had been sent to Tres Piedras railroad station, eighteen miles away, to bring loads, and then to take guests, orchestra and chef back. It was wonderful how he had managed it all in three days

For a month we traveled, visiting different cities. In Los Angeles we had our wedding picture taken at a fine studio. Were we still tired from all the work and excitement that we looked so serious? It was so different from the smiling brides I now see in photographs. Nevertheless, we were just as happy.

At the Palace Hotel in San Francisco the guide from the hotel took us one evening through Chinatown. He showed us the Chinese Temple, the opium fiends' quarters and a banquet hall filled with elegantly attired guests in richly embroidered silk robes. At the theater we were seated in the place of honor, on the stage with the actors.

Returning to Los Angeles we visited Catalina Island and Santa Barbara. For hours we sat in silent wonder on seashores watching the waves rolling over the immense tur-

81

quoise blue sea, to break into foamy cataracts on dazzling sand stretches. The old missions we found interesting too, but our pleasant trip must now come to an end.

On our way back we stopped at Las Vegas at the new Castañeda Hotel. Ven called up some of his friends and at once we were showered with invitations to dinners, teas and evening parties — at the homes of ex-Governor Larrazolo, Dr. Hernandez, Don Eusebio Chacon, Jose Baca, Jr., and Doña Doloritas, his mother. This was one of those never to be forgotten homes and hearthstones of the days of the rich Dons in New Mexico, full of that traditional Spanish hospitality. Some time ago I read in the *New Mexico Magazine* an article entitled "New Mexico Landmarks." It gave a very interesting description of this attractive home and its rich furnishings, telling how they had been hauled from the States by ox teams over the famous Santa Fe Trail.

Arriving in Santa Fe, we were invited to dinners at Governor Otero's, Judge McFie's and Senator Spiese's homes.

Finally the round of invitations ended, and we boarded our little railroad, the D.&R.G., on our way home.

CHAPTER XIII

At the Home I Found
Difficult to Call Home

It was almost twilight when we entered the El Rito village, steeped in dead silence, with a few lights beginning to twinkle in high windows. The Jaramillos' house seemed deserted when we arrived. We walked along the long front porch and through the front hall to the back porch. There we found Ven's mother and his grandmother, Melita, sitting at a supper table placed under the kitchen window out on the back porch. Florencia, the maid, was handing them the dishes through the window. Old Refugio, whom Ven's sisters called "the witch," was squatting on the porch floor against the kitchen door. They got up to greet us, and we went in to get washed and came out to join them at a scanty supper of roasted lamb ribs, fried potatoes, coffee and rolls. A dry rib and roll was all I could eat of this, and I felt so weak and hungry, after the rough, all-day ride that shook one quite empty. Leaving the table, my mother-in-law showed us the bedroom and living room they had fixed up for us with the furniture I had bought and sent from Denver with the check my father gave me as a wedding present. Ven went up town to get the mail. Left alone I felt so lonely. This quiet, dim house was now to be my home. I was trying to keep back the tears when a dismal cry made me spring up

83

in terror to lock the door. Another unearthly cry echoed through the hills. A woman in distress, perhaps beaten and thrown out of her home by a drunken husband, has come to take refuge down here in the wooded river, I thought. Ven, returning with the mail and finding the door locked, asked, "Afraid, mi vida?" "Oh, the most awful wailing that I have ever heard from the river," I said. "Just a coyote announcing a change of weather, Pedro would tell you. The hungry beasts come after my fat lambs in the corral, and one coyote howl sounds like a herd of them," Ven said. The lonely cry haunted me after I went to bed, and I lay awake listening to the cheery crickets in the garden and the gurgling croak of the frogs in the pond by the river. This would be the music I would hear from now on, every night.

Sunday came. There is something about this day that makes it alike everywhere, peaceful, quiet, but more so here, after the church services when the people went back to their farms. In the afternoon my living room filled with guests who called to meet Venceslao's wife. This must have been an established custom, for my mother-in-law had refreshments ready and helped Florencia, the maid, pass them to the guests, who sat around the room very quietly. I felt relieved when my sister-in-law, who was always ready for lively conversation, came in and told a little amusing story about Pablita, who had been Mrs. Grant's maid.

The guests had a good laugh at the joke on Pablita. This released the tension and started conversation.

Several weeks later, while returning a call, with Ven's mother, at the big mansion of the wealthy Don Romolo Martinez (a relative), where old formalities still reigned, the maid passed to us the accustomed refreshments. I took a swallow of what I thought was Angelica wine, and my breath caught and tears filled my eyes. It was strong whisky, which I had never tasted in my life. Scared and embarrassed I handed the wine cup back to the maid, just as Don Romulo came in the room and with a formal embrace, but warm salutation, greeted his *comadre,* Ana Maria. She turned and introduced me, and I stood charmed by this white-bearded gentleman still practicing the genteel manners of the Spanish Dons of old. *"Mi tatita,"* his youngest daughter called this tall, broad-shouldered, hardy-looking pioneer.

CHAPTER XIV

Memories at the Old Home

A few weeks after our return from California, my husband guessing my homesickness, said: "If you want to go to see your folks, Gabriel can take you to Barranca." I cheered up, and early next morning was on my way to the railroad station. Over hills and through sandy arroyos the team plodded. The sandy road caught the merciless glare of the hot sun's rays, flourishing them back at us. The heaving, sweat-denched horses stopped every few paces to take a breath. It took four hours before we came in sight of the frame depot. Then came a long hour wait before I was at last comfortably seated on a red plush cushioned seat on the day coach of the D. & R. G. In winter the car was heated by coal stoves and lit at night with acetylene lamps. Our "Chili Line," as it was called, did not make much speed; however, by three o'clock I disembarked at Tres Piedras station and took my seat by my oldest brother on our small buggy. Travel over this hard road was easier, but so eager was I with happy anticipation to see my family, that the eighteen-mile ride over the sage-covered plain that appeared unbroken to the base of the distant mountains, seemed endless. Suddenly we found ourselves at the brink of the chasm of the Rio Grande canyon. In those days the descent of this steep, deep canyon over a narrow, rock trail was thrilling adventure that held the breath of those that were not used to it as we were. The

MEMORIES AT THE OLD HOME

sun was sinking behind us when we came to the foot of the
steep road, crossed the toll bridge and ascended the less steep
canyon of the Arroyo Hondo River and came in view of the
high peaks of the Sangre de Cristo on the east, now bathed
in the rosy hues that gave it its name.

A hymn of gladness sang in my heart as we came in sight
of the villages nestling in their natural setting at the foot of
the high ridges of hills that shelter the green bowl of the
valley. It appeared like an oasis in a desert after the ride
across the plain. To the quietness of the evening, shedding
its peace and serenity on the inhabitants, the meadowlarks,
charas and *tildios* added their sweet vesper songs from the
meadows along the river.

As we swung in between the adobe houses in the main
village, the aromatic smoke of burning *piñon* and cedar
wood, circling out of low chimneys, filled the air. In open
doors stood familiar faces smiling a *"Como le va, comadrita?"*

My family received me with open arms. Relatives and
friends called to see me. Even old Romulo came from Arroyo Seco, bringing my mother a gift of two pairs of baby
socks that his wife had knitted from the lambs' wool. .

"That was the biggest wedding they had in Taos this
summer when the governor's daughter got married," he said.
"Were you invited?" mother asked. "No, but I went to get
a look at the governor, and got also a taste of the fine wines
through the hotel back kitchen door," he answered. Mother
smiled a, "Yes, it was a big wedding."

I returned calls in the afternoons, and in the evenings,
as of old, I took my rounds of the orchard grounds, listening
to the shrill songs of the blackbird flocks lining the standing
cedar post fence. Back of the fence ran the mother ditch,
banked with drooping willows and wild flowers. The lambs
and cows lowing, stopped to take a drink of the crystalline
water. Erineo's chore at each day's closing was to bring them
in from the meadow where they had been feasting on fragrant herbs and grass.

Far away across the river, dogs barked, children yelled
happily at play in cool patios. Vivid memories carried me

87

back to the yesteryears, recalling the times in my girlhood when I had lived so happily among these people for whom I had an inherent love, to the times when dressed up in starched, ruffled dress, I went with them, through their happy feast days and religious ceremonies, kneeling on the ground, answering their hymns and prayers, with the same faith and fervor as theirs. Oh, time, turn back and let me live again, just for a minute, those happy days!

With regret I tore myself from these happy dreams to go in and join the family at evening prayers. At the end, each one of us children knelt before my mother to receive her blessing and kiss her hand before retiring.

Through the open window in my bedroom came the moonlight and the shadow of the capilla chapel tower, the splash of the river water, the murmuring of the ditch water circling the orchard grounds, lulling me to sleep dreamless and sound.

My happy visit ended too soon. In two weeks I was parting with my dear family and on my way back to the home that had only my husband's love to attract me. But that had the substance of being enough, although I missed that happy busy bustle and hustle we had at my home.

Early in the morning I was again riding across the extensive, desolate plain. In the far distance the tremendous mountain ranges hovered on the horizon like purple guardians. The silent solemnity reigning over all filled my young mind with wonder at the power and wisdom that had created it. The thought comforted me.

My good husband, always with the thought of my comfort at heart and wishing to give me a surprise on my return, had fixed a large, sunny dining room and kitchen out of the room that had served as his father's store. It had been full of boxes of squashy, old-fashioned hats, mufflers and other junk. He had the walls papered in pretty blue and the woodwork painted white. The double door was turned into a wide, deep-silled window in the dining room. This pleased me most, for I could fill it with plants.

Tomasa, whom I had brought with me for my maid, now

came in handy as a cook, for she could do both. Ven's mother at once closed their kitchen, and she and her mother came to board with us, as they did not have a cook. His two sisters, who were disappointed because their brother had not married a girl of their choice, did not feel friendly enough to come to my table; but their mother had the temerity, as soon as a meal was ready, to come in, pick out the choicest portions and send them on a tray to the girls' room. I stood this unpleasant situation for some time, until one morning in the fall, when the flocks of wild ducks were taking their flight to the south, my husband took his gun and went down to the pond and returned with two ducks. Through hard study I prepared them by a recipe in my cook book, and waited for Ven to come home to show him proudly the culinary accomplishments I was acquiring. When Tomasa set the platter before him at the table with only the smallest duck on it, I watched him carving small pieces, trying to make it go around to the four of us. He passed me my plate. I got up and left the table. He of course followed me to my room to find out what was the matter. "Nothing, but I want my own home," I said, and burst out crying. "You shall have it," Ven answered soothingly.

He must have been as anxious as I was to have our own home, where he could invite his friends to visit or stop when they came to town. I recall about one evening when Dr. Martin, one of the men who had so generously thrown his home open to help house our wedding guests, stopped in to see Ven. He sat in the office for a while and then got up saying: "I better go up town and try and find a room for myself and my driver. He is outside waiting for me." I knew how embarrassed Ven must have felt at not being able to ask him to stay. But we only had our living room and bedroom; the rest of the big house his sisters bossed, and that year they had not opened the summer and guest quarters but were using just the little winter kitchenette with no dining room. We could not very well entertain guests in such poor accommodations. In two weeks the foundations of the eight-room house I planned were going up, regardless of all the

89

grumbling going on. The grandmother, who could never resign herself to Ven's modern extravagance, saw no need of building another big house.

My eight rooms finished, Ven thought of adding a second story. Seeing him so determined, I resigned myself to his wishes and showed the builder a picture I had of a house built with a balcony running all around the second story. Four bedrooms and a flower room were added upstairs, opening onto this balcony. That left the large reception hall in the center opened to the ceiling of the second story, in the style of some of the hotel lobbies I had seen.

In December, when wintry cold weather set in and the building work had to stop, my husband decided to take a trip east. Before leaving, we conceived the idea of having a Christmas tree for the village children. We set a tree in the open dining room and brought in an organ, and I invited some of the girls to help me sing some Christmas songs. It would be fun to have a Santa Claus, so we dressed the priest, Father Alvern, as Santa. The carpenters nailed boards across the hall for seats. Everything went on beautifully until Santa came out. The children had never seen the white-whiskered old Santa before. They became so frightened that they yelled and cried, hanging on to their mothers. Older boys up on the balcony ran down yelling, almost upsetting the oil lamps set on the stairway. In the commotion, the board seats gave way, catching some of the people's feet under them. More screams and cries. Finally my husband came in and began distributing the toys and candy. The crying ceased, quiet was restored, and everyone left smiling and happy.

CHAPTER XV

First Trip East

We soon were ready to start on our trip. In Chicago we
stopped at the lakeside Auditorium Hotel for a day's rest,
then went on to New York City. We arrived there about
nine o'clock in the evening, and my husband did something
he had never done before, even in the well-known city of
Denver. He took the street car to the St. Dennis Hotel. We
stood in the cold, waiting to transfer, and finally reached the
hotel only to find it filled with guests.

We tried another place with the same results. Ven remembered the Cumberland Hotel, a small family hotel Mr.
Stabb had told him about. We drove there and found a front
room, facing the giant Waldorf-Astoria on Park Avenue.
Anxious to see that grand, famous hotel, the following
evening we dressed up and went to have dinner there. Ladies
in formal evening gowns and men in full-dress suits filled
the dining rooms. The stiff, white-collared French waiter
set a menu card before us. I glanced down the list of French
names. "Bouquetiers, Bourgriegusone, etc." I could not
make out what a single name meant. "Order anything you
like," I said with cool reserve, concealing my ignorance.
"What about oyster stew?" Ven asked. He was especially
fond of oysters. This course finished, he looked at the card
again. "Strawberries from the Bermudas. Just think of it in
January. Let's have some." The waiter placed before Ven

the luscious berries spilling out of a pretty china "horn of plenty" into a lace-covered silver dish, a pile of snowy whipped cream on the side. "These are delicious," I said, adding in Spanish: "I wonder what the waiter thinks of this *principio y fin!*" (this beginning and ending).

We were invited to dinners at our friends, the Browns; and one evening went over the Brooklyn Bridge, spanning the East River, to a fine, planked-fish dinner at the Grants. Next day we took a ride through Central Park in one of the funniest little automobiles first invented. The driver sat on a high seat at the back, guiding the car looking over the top. Two low doors enclosed us in a narrow seat in front. At every turn, I felt as if I would fall out, and held onto Ven's arm. We stopped at the Madison Square Gardens dog show, and bought a blue-ribboned black Spaniel named "Gladdies." The name suited perfectly; she was the happiest little dog — always met me at the gate, bouncing all over me. There were beautiful Newfoundlands, and St. Bernards belonging to the millionaire Goulds and Vanderbilts. Next we took the ferry boat to Bedloe's Island to see the Statue of Liberty. We rode on the elevator with the guide as far as the head of the statue, and from there climbed a winding stairway to the top of the torch. I shuddered when the guide told us that the ashes on the loophole windows we were looking out through were ashes of a man who had requested that his ashes be blown over the ocean from there. We took a ride on the elevated train just to see what it was like, and on the underground subway we rode to the Navy Yards. How Ven obtained passes I don't know, but we went through the gates and saw sailors loading a war vessel. We went to the Stock Exchange on Wall Street and to the art museum. In the evenings we took in the opera and some of the Shakespeare plays, "Julius Caesar," "Macbeth" and "The Merchant of Venice." At the Old Knickerbocker, Maude Adams was playing in "L'Aiglon," as the son of Napoleon. She wore a military coat trimmed in solid fourteen-carat gold buttons and trimmings said to have cost $1,350. "Floradora," a pretty light opera, we saw at another theater.

FIRST TRIP EAST

On the third of March we were speeding on the Pennsylvania Railroad down to Washington to attend President McKinley's inaguration. Mrs. Rodey and Judge Rodey — he was then a delagate to Congress from the territory of New Mexico — met us at the railroad station and took us to a hotel where he had been fortunate to find a room for us that had two windows facing Pennsylvania Avenue, down which the inaguaral parade would pass the following day.

By ten o'clock in the morning on the fourth of March, the sidewalks along the avenue were crowded with people. Some had their camp stools and lunch with them. Others fainted from standing so long. Ven had ordered four lunches sent up to the room when we came in with Judge and Mrs. Rodey from the inaugural ceremony at the capital. Between runs to the windows we managed to eat a few bites. Preceding the parade, as a personal escort, came the Black Horses Troop of Cleveland, then one hundred veterans of the 23rd Ohio Volunteers, and as special mounted aides, the five ex-Presidents' sons. The Marine Band, the West Point and the Annapolis cadets — so well drilled, with every square shoulder and foot evenly in line — more military detachments and bands followed. An imposing sight it was, to be long remembered. Judge Rodey had obtained tickets for the Inaugural Ball and other functions. The Grand Ball that night in the Pension building was a gorgeous affair. The all-spangled or sequin and beaded gowns, which had just come in style, lent a regal splendor to the brilliant gathering.

At midnight, Judge and Mrs. Rodey took us to dinner. Big oysters in the shell on ice were served as first course. I pretended I was enjoying them, but could not break off the tiniest piece. I noticed Ven's plate with only one oyster left on it, and asked him when we reached our room: "How in the world do you eat those awful raw oysters?" "You roll them on your fork and let them slide down," he advised. I wanted to try that, but was afraid I would choke.

Before we left the city we visited the Smithsonian Institute, Corcoran Gallery, the Senate and House of Representatives, the White House and Mount Vernon.

ROMANCE OF A LITTLE VILLAGE GIRL

From Washington we went to Buffalo. The Pan American Fair was not yet opened, but the buildings were already finished. Six months later, the President was assassinated while attending this fair. The Niagara Falls we had visited earlier in the winter when the trees, grounds and water were frozen. What a magnificent sight it was.

On our return trip, Ven had to remain in Denver to attend to some business matters and I went ahead to stop and visit my mother in Taos. Ven placed me in the Pullman car and left. Early next morning when the porter announced breakfast at Salida, I was not through dressing, knowing that the train usually did not stop for breakfast until it reached Alamosa. I rushed and got to the dining car. When I return I noticed I was in a different car, and asked the porter. He answered: "That car went to Salt Lake City." I became frantic. My alligator traveling bag, with my jewels in it, had gone in that car. What would Ven think? On my very first trip alone, I could not take care of my things. Alamosa was the next stop. I rushed to the depot and wired Ven: "Lost satchel with jewels at Salida. Went in car to Salt Lake City." The day after, an article came out in the *Denver Post* with this headline: "Bride loses precious gems, the Denver pawnshops will be searched." Young Jaramillo, the husband, called at police headquarters, puffing a cigarette and saying indignantly, "This world is full of scoundrels. Who dares rob a young bride?" The car, after being sidetracked for two days, returned to Denver, and my satchel was found untouched between the backs of two seats where I had left it.

Ven was his grandmother's favorite grandson. She had raised him from the time he was a few months old, when his father became desperate about trying to raise the delicate baby and packed the boy up and took him to his mother-in-law, Grandma Melita. She was an able manager, and Juliana, the big, fat Navajo maid, was assigned as his nurse. Seven years later, when his father went to Abiquiu to get his son so as to send him to boarding school, he was delighted at the good job the grandmother and Juliana had done.

Several years after this the grandmother, Melita, broke up her home and took turns living with her daughters. She kept her two most valuable possessions, her gold filigree, emerald-set necklace and her hand-hammered silverplate. Her daughters begged her to give these possessions to them, but no, they were for the girl who would marry Venceslao. I was the lucky girl who received them as wedding presents.

Juliana — *"Abuela"* ("Grannie"), all the family called her — was now living with her son, but she was such a good-natured, faithful soul, she never forgot to come once in a while to pay a visit to her mistress. She was treated as company and only went into the kitchen to prepare some special dish. She would watch until she saw Ven come home; then she would go plodding down our sidewalk, like a fat duck out of water, holding a nice dish, which was her pride to set before Ven at the table. She left with a happy smile when he praised her good cooking.

How Ven was spoiled by the whole family, being the only boy.

Grandma Melita's husband was the former Don Pablo Gallegos, once owner of the old La Fonda Inn at the end of the Santa Fe Trail. When he sold the inn, banks were still unknown in New Mexico, and so he took the pot of gold and buried it in one of the rooms in his home at Abiquiu. Mama Melita and her five handsome daughters showed, in their dignified proud bearing, aristocratic traits. Aunt Piedad was one of the daughters. Mama Melita was a strict disciplinarian, accustomed to managing a large household and many Indian slaves. Although seemingly very serious, there was a hidden humorous wit in her, displayed often in her conversation. Religious tradition ruled in her home. All the family, including servants, had to join in prayers in her room. It was her custom the first thing at the start of a trip to recite the long rosary and other prayers, to which we all answered.

ROMANCE OF A LITTLE VILLAGE GIRL

"Home." What a beautiful word! Our home was the center of the universe, enshrined in our hearts with ties of love, and where happiness and peaceful harmony always reigned. The eve of the 4th of July, Ven and I moved into our new home, and next morning hung out on our front porch the stars and stripes, for my husband was very patriotic.

The house was attractive and lovely. Two carpenters had lavished their skill in the paneling, railings and grill-work. Sam, the painter, had added his artistic talent in penciling wood shades from deep mahogany to cherry red. The wallpaper was of the most attractive and expensive patterns. Little stained glasses surrounding the large panes added color to dining room and parlor windows. Altogether it was an elaborate house with a broad view of green fields, wooded river and purple mountains. It was not so badly planned by two inexperienced twenty-year-olds.

The first thing we did was to invite relatives and friends to come to a housewarming party. The dance was held in the wide hall with the dining room opening into it. Ven, who could not waltz a step, had great fun calling out the figures in the newly-introduced square dance, the lancers, in a loud voice. "First couple to the right, four hands around, swing your partner, all join hands circle to the right," quickly changing to the left, etc. It was no small feat not to get confused in the fast, intricate figures. The mix-ups caused great fun. This was a pleasant change from the quiet, dignified Spanish dances. Many guests came to the party and continued to drop in whenever they came to town, sometimes right at meal times. The stores then did not carry groceries like they do now. In a hurry I had to help the cook bake a pan of biscuits and prepare a company's meal. Carmen, my cook, was a Utah slave whom Uncle Gaspar bought from the Indians with a team of mules. Trained in his household, she was the best cook and so neat. She always changed her kitchen apron to a white one to serve the table, even when we did not have guests. The friends we invited to visit us found our home so pleasant that some of them remained for months. This happened with three Denver girls who came in September and remained for two months. When friends from the Springs or other places dropped in, we played games and sang songs. They were free to roll up the rugs in the large hall and dance to the *pianola* music. Ven's youngest sister, Annette, had married a nice, friendly boy, and they would also come and join in the fun. Once, seeing Tony Joseph throwing the rugs out on the porch, she remarked: "I bet you Tony does not tear up his house like this." I thought to myself, what is the use of having a nice home if we cannot enjoy it, and share it with our friends? Others kept their nice guest rooms locked up until the fine carpets got full of moths, but I had been reared in a home where guests were always welcomed.

The fall was the most beautiful of the seasons. After the rumble of heavy wagons bringing in the harvest quieted down, a peaceful quiet settled through the valley. Store rooms now filled with winter supplies. With a feeling of plenty and ease, the people's minds then turned to rest and pleasure. Weddings with dancing and feasting took place. One night we took our girl friends on a hay ride down to the lower village to one of these dances in a hall with a mud floor. They remarked that the people did not seem to be enjoying themselves, that they all looked so serious. There was none of that chatting nor smiling with the partner as there is now. Everyone was quiet and reserved in those days.

Before the parish feast of St. John of Nepomuc, in October, my husband said: "You girls make a list of good eats for a nice *fiesta* dinner, and I will invite the priests to come." The list they handed Ven was a long one of the very best things. The girls helped prepare the dinner. The four priests came and the fine dinner was greatly enjoyed, but when the $25 grocery bill came, I was shocked.

The girls, teeming with sparkling Irish wit, were entertaining and we enjoyed their company, but at last my generous husband became tired of footing the bill. One day while joking, he asked, "And when are you girls going

97

home?" Not a bit ruffled one of them answered, "When you get us a pass." Members of the legislature were then given free railroad passes. Ven obtained passes for the three and they left, having added a few pounds to their weight with the rest and healthy country climate. A young couple brought a few-months-old baby and visited us a month. I furnished even a nurse for the baby.

When election time came, Grandma Melita's prophecy came true. She had finally arrived at the conclusion that Ven was building such a big home to house his political *recoleras,* meetings. For the convention, Ven played host to all the candidates running on the ticket, from the governor down to our county officials.

The spring season arrived, and with it the many activities of a busy farm and country estate started. Ven took great pride in the improvement of his village. After directing the planting of the farms, the lambing and the shearing of the sheep, the building of some new building or remodeling of one started. The old church was repaired from roof to foundation. I still love the sound of the hammer and lumber, and later, in July, the whirring of the hay mower, the odor of freshly-cut alfalfa and the merry chatter of the peons. When Ven called them to come for a cup of coffee, they first crowded around the well to take a drink of cool water. They all drank from the same cup with no fear of germs. Then they sat along the sidewalk, along the shady side of the house, wiping the drops of perspiration that ran down their red, hot brows, while the cook passed them a large pot of hot coffee and a tray of freshly-baked biscuits. Like the soil they toiled, these men were tan and sturdy. Ven came in the dining room for his eggnog and cake. Refreshed, the men went back to work until sunset. Ven sat perched up on the fence watching them. When any of the men did something annoying he would say with so much patience: *"Dios te bendiga* (God bless you), Ramos, or Juan," whomever he spoke to.

FIRST TRIP EAST

The St. Louis World Fair had opened in the fall, and Ven and Jack, his brother-in-law, thinking they would be too busy to attend, gave Annette and me a pocketbook full of money and sent us off to the fair. Not finding rooms at the inn in the fair grounds, we had to stop at a hotel in town and take a cab back and forth. Afraid to take the ride after dark, we would leave the fair grounds early, and missed the greatest fun on the Pike. Tired of going around alone, in a week's time we had seen all we cared to see, and spent the rest of our money shopping. I bought a long beaver fur collarette at the Siberia building and a twenty-dollar hat to match at a downtown store. We felt very happy with our new outfits. Later, Ven and Jack found time to go. They found themselves with a group of New Mexico relatives and friends visiting the fair, and had a very grand time. The illuminations and gondolas on the lake were the prettiest sights.

CHAPTER XVI

An Enchanting Trip

My mother's health broke down from keeping so close at work, and her doctor advised a change to a warmer climate. I was delighted when she wrote asking me to join them on a trip to Mexico. With my father and little sister, we started in November for El Paso, rested a day there, and went on to Chihuahua, the city my mother had always desired to visit, as it was connected with a romantic incident of her mother's and father's marriage.

During the picturesque days of the caravan, her father, Jesus Maria Lucero, while traveling in a caravan led by his brother-in-law, Don Gasper Ortiz, met his bride at a hacienda, well on the outskirts of the city of Chihuahua. They were on their way to Durango, and on their return, mother's father had insisted that Don Gaspar accompany him to the *señorita's* home to ask for her in marriage. Doña Refugio, the mother, had already known of Don Gaspar, and the proposal was accepted. A quiet wedding took place in the imposing Chihuahua Cathedral, noted for its beautiful sculptured front. Then the caravan continued on its way to the north, escorting a coach with the newlyweds, the mother and the Indian maid. For weeks they rode through the lonely trail of *La Jornada del Muerto,* marked with many crude graves of massacred victims of murderous Indians. At night the timid bride heard the men around the campfire telling terrifying stories of these Indians raids, but good luck favored them this time and the weary travelers reached Santa Fe safely.

Our visit in Chihuahua was during the holidays preceding the feast of Our Lady of Guadalupe, which is observed throughout Mexico for a week, with open gambling and feasting, right out in booths built on the street leading to the *Santuario*.

Chihuahua is an ancient city. In the hotel where we stopped, the thick stone steps were so deeply worn out in the center that we had to walk up on the sides. Taking a ride around the city the driver pointed out to us the white mansions of the millionaire, Don Luis Terrazas, and of his son-in-law, Mr. Creele. Out on the lawn was a nurse, in full uniform, watching the two Creele boys at play. About two miles out was Mr. Terraza's white *finca*. Peering through open *saguan* doors we caught glimpses of grilled iron balconies and frescoed walls.

Our next stop was at the Hotel de la Cueva, in Santa Rosalia, for a week's rest and baths in the mineral springs, then on to *Aguas Calientes,* the center of drawn work. The *socalo* (park) was the most beautiful we saw throughout Mexico. Each town had its own distinctive type of art. Guadalajara's pottery is famous; fine blankets, baskets, feather pictures and flowers were shown at other places. At Queretaro boys came to the Pullman car window selling round boxes of rich *cajeta.* The mining town of Zacatecas looked like an ant city. The streets and even house yards were full of earth mounds. From there on, the vegetation became more verdant. White-towered churches and white buildings furnished contrast to the color scheme of subtropical foliage, green landscaping and big maguey plantations.

Soon we found ourselves in the metropolis, the city of Mexico. Here we found good accommodations at the small Porter's Hotel, managed by an American couple. The food was good but the rooms were dark and cool. A little girl at the hotel told me: "When we are cold, we go to bed." But we were there to see the country, and warmed ourselves

101

by getting out in the sun. After a quiet Christmas, we left for Cuernavaca. From a high mountain altitude the road looped down to a few feet above sea level, and we found ourselves in an ideal climate. The semi-tropical position of the city gives it an even June-like temperature throughout the year. One has to see Cuernavaca to succumb to the charm of its antique picturesqueness. This city dates back to the time of Cortez, 1529. I was at once fascinated, beginning with the ride from the railroad station in a little antiquated car pulled by a team of burros over a one-iron rail. The white-clad driver, a true Aztec type, flicked his lazy team with his long leather whip often, and blew the whistle in his mouth at every turn of the road. The car stopped at the entrance of the *socalo,* and the passengers were met there by the bellboys from the hotels, to carry the baggage. The three hotels were under American management. The Morelos, where we lodged, I figured, must have been built by some Spanish grandee who had large wealth to build such a costly building. The long salons were now used as dining rooms; broad stone stairways led up to two stories of arched porches and to a roof garden. Glass French doors opened into iron-railed balconies.

Sitting in the cool shade of the porches, inhaling the air that was heavy laden with perfume from flowers in hanging baskets and flower beds, and potted roses, ferns and palms hiding the fountain in the center court, we listened to the children in the adjoining building singing their lessons while they learned. This method of teaching, introduced in the Sixteenth Century, was still used. In the gathering dusk of the evening we sat in the roof garden listening to the band concert and watching the crowd of people circling around the park, the line of women on the inside promenading in one direction, the men on the outside going in the opposite. This gave the boys a chance to direct enamored glances to their sweethearts as they passed each other. Speaking the same language, with a natural sympathy and understanding of the people in this our neighbor country, we of course at once caught the essence, and reveled in their customs, their gentle, polite manner practiced even by the poor uneducated class, their traditions and history, and in the fabulous elaborate buildings, ancient cathedrals and quaint markets.

A block from the hotel was the Palace of Cortez, then used as the capitol. Amid blooming oleander and citrus fruit trees rose a grey monument to the memory of the intrepid Cortez. Inside, the walls were covered with large pictures of Iturbides, Hidalgo and other famous generals in their gorgeous uniforms, showing their proud Spanish heritage. In the seclusion of the *Jardin de La Borda,* which is said to have cost the millionaire silver miner, La Borda, a million dollars, we found restful retreat. In the garden were fountains, terraces, a small lake and all kinds of tropical plants and trees. We raved about the blooming poinsettias four feet high. Down by the river were seen women bent over smooth stones scrubbing their clothes. The public market was a busy place of great interest; there one learned to know Mexico and its native people, especially on the days that herds of burros brought in supplies from the country farms. There was a public bath house in a pretty garden, with baths from ten cents up to fifty cents, first, second and third class.

Cuernavaca is a city of churches. In the same square was a group of three churches, magnificent structures, constructed in the wonderful architecture of the Sixteenth Century. Across the street rose the white-towered chapel of El Calvario. Faith and reverence dwelt within their white walls.

When we were about to return home, my husband wrote that he would wait for us at the capital. I answered, "No, you must come down here." I wanted him to see this ancient city that reminded me so much of pictures I had seen of Jerusalem, with its narrow, tilted, cobble-stoned streets, red-tiled roofs and round white church towers. He came and found it most interesting. While attending school at Regis College in Denver he had known the two Reina boys from Cuernavaca. One evening, at a church *hamaic*a (bazaar), we met one of these boys and his wife.

ROMANCE OF A LITTLE VILLAGE GIRL

On an afternoon while the priest was holding the ceremony of blessing the animals and seeds, and the church yard was full of people — some holding baskets of seeds, women holding hens, boys with a rooster or pigeon tucked under their arms — *mozos* led in by the bridle a team of fine-bred horses owned by this man Reina. The horses were so spirited everybody had to move out of the way.

Another day, Ven asked the *mozo* door-keeper to hire five burros for us. Promptly after breakfast, the driver with the burros was at the hotel door. Decked in broad-brimmed Mexican hats, the five of us started on a ride to Acatzingo, to see the ruins of Emperor Maximilian's house. Through a very narrow trail the driver led our burros, sometimes pulling each one by the bridle down steep, rocky places, with us holding tight to our saddles and hats. At noon we reached the ruins of what must have been a very small village, and very little remains of an adobe house that the guide pointed out as Maximilian's house. We ate the lunch that Rosa had put up for us at the hotel, and started back, reaching the city at dusk, hungry and tired, but still amused at the thought of dignified father and mother riding on burros.

Back at the capital, I found my trunk which had been sent by mistake to the wrong address. Now that I had my nice clothes with me, I called up my friends, Miss Ortiz and the Perrons, whose wedding I had attended in Denver while they were there on a trip through the States with their family, before they sailed for Europe.

In this metropolis the rich lived with great formality. We were invited to a very rich luncheon at the Perron's beautiful home. Miss Ortiz made us a formal call, inviting us to what she called *unos tamalitos*.

By six o'clock in the evening, Ven was using the heavy, iron knocker on the high, carved *saguan* door of the Ortiz home. A white-clad boy opened one of the leaves on the double door and asked us, "Shall I announce you?" Receiving an affirmative answer, he pulled a cord by the stairway column and a gong rang in the balcony above. By the time we reached the top of the stairs, Miss Ortiz was awaiting us with a warm greeting. She ushered us into a salon furnished in the formal, elegant fashion of the best Latin society. Her two sisters, Sara and Biatriz, were introduced. Miss Ortiz (now Mrs. Burns) is gifted with the most graceful, stately poise and attractive personality of any woman I have ever known, and is a charming entertainer; but seven o'clock, eight o'clock passed, and I began feeling pretty faint and tired. Miss Ortiz had visited in our home and knew our rule of early dinner. "Let's go in and start on the dinner," she said, leading the way to the dining room. "Something is delaying my mother on her visit to her sister."

The simple *tamalitos* proved to be a full six-course dinner. The mother, handsome and dignified, finally arrived, apologizing. At nine o'clock, in the middle of the dinner, the taxi cab called to take us back to the hotel. My husband sent the driver word to return in half an hour. I was embarrassed to leave just a few minutes after we had left the table. I knew, but had forgotten, about the Mexican custom of late dinners.

I also forgot about the church rule of women to the right and men to the left. One Sunday noon coming from the concert at the Alameda, where the fashionable strolled while the band played, passing by the church of St. Francis, I noticed a line of elegant victorias and coaches standing in front. Curious to find out what was going on at this unusual hour for services, I went in. Noticing room for one in one of the pews to the left, I took it. Why were the ladies across the aisle looking at me so strangely? Noticing the pews on that side were filled with men only, I got up, embarrassed, and left the seat church at once. This turned more eyes on me, making me feel still more embarrassed.

Every evening at seven o'clock we sat in front of the Porter's Hotel watching the parade of elegantly equipped carriages, drawn by fine-bred, prancing horses, passing on the way to the *Paseo de la Reforma*, (the grand avenue). The footman and driver in high silk hats, the jeweled ladies elegantly attired and sitting so proudly, with sprays of fresh poinsettias at their feet or on the seat before them. *"Flor de Navidad"* they call it, and have a pretty legend connected with this flower.

We were amazed at the elaborate sculpture of the antique buildings and artistic frescoes and the grandeur of avenues. The cathedral stood in surpassing grandeur facing the *socalo.* It's a world in itself, full of faith and piety. Class distinction, so prominent through the country, is ignored here. The peon in coarse garments kneels with gentry clad in costly clothes. It is an inspiring witness of the faith of the Mexican people. The same faith is found at the rich Basilica of Guadalupe. This is a silver treasure house, with its solid silver railings, chandeliers and altar candelabras.

Out on the suburbs we saw the *Arbol de la Noche Triste,* the tree of great antiquity under which Cortez shed tears that eventful, sad night when the Aztecs rose in arms and massacred his brave soldiers. The tree had only a few branches still alive.

A ride to Chapultupec, the president's palace, and a boat ride on the Viga to the floating gardens at Xochimilco, and our trip ended here.

After another week's rest at Santa Rosalia mineral springs and at Chihuahua, we turned our steps homeward.

Five months' rest in this languid, exotic land of leisure that lies drowsing under scorching suns, in this paradise of souls, where the sole ambition of most is to obtain just enough for their daily needs, had restored my mother's strength sufficiently to fight her ills for a number of years after.

CHAPTER XVII

A Happy Surprise

For ten years we had lived in almost perfect happiness, traveling half the time, visiting cities, fairs and other amusement places. Our lives ran always smoothly. Neither of us had a temper. We were united in all our ideas; there was no arguing, no meddling, both doing as we pleased without having to consult the other. I often thought of what I heard Cicilio, Aunt Magdalena's cook, say, about a month after he was married: he was so happy, that if it were true that there was a chair in heaven for the couple who did not regret having married, he and his wife were going to occupy it. I thought Saint Peter would have to buy another chair when Ven and I got there.

At the end of those ten years of an unworried life a happy surprise was coming to us. With great preparations I went to a Denver hospital in the month of December. Ven engaged the most noted obstetrical specialist. The English nurse he recommended had an England and Denver certificate, and was supposed to be one of the best. Two weeks before the scheduled time of the happy event I was at the Mercy Hospital under their care. Two days before Christmas the stork brought us a sweet baby boy. "What a perfect model," the doctor exclaimed when he saw him. Do babies have happy dreams? He seemed always smiling in his sleep, or was it an angel's smile?

ROMANCE OF A LITTLE VILLAGE GIRL

Ven's and my joy were without bounds. He went downtown dressed up in a new suit and a stiff derby hat, and came back with the happiest smile, carrying a box of flowers. However, our joy was of short duration. Five days later our baby had parted from us and left us brokenhearted.

On the second day, when the nurse brought in the baby from his bath, I felt his little hands and they were ice cold. "The baby is so cold," I said to her. "Just on the outside," she answered, putting the baby back in his basket up on the table by the window. I almost cried. I wanted to keep him by me, to keep him warm.

By next day his kidneys had stopped functioning. The baby specialist called in circumcised the baby as a cure. He cut a blood vessel and the baby bled to death.

CHAPTER XVIII

Back at the Country Home

Always when I returned to my home from a trip, our good neighbors came to see me. Hearing what had happened to our baby, the *medica* said: "That trouble comes from catching cold. We roast an onion, split it open, and while it is still warm, place it over the baby's bladder. *Muy pronto* (very soon), the functioning is released."

That summer I busied myself in my garden with my flowers, to drown my sorrow. There is a romance in gardening. The mere word makes me think of bright sunshine, of flower-scented air. To bury a dry seed in the ground and see it burst through the earth as a green sprout, watch it grow, spread its branches and be covered with exquisite flowers, is a magic wand.

The rock garden in the center of my lawn was my pride. I had ridden up to the Red Bluffs in my phaeton, followed by Sofio in the wagon, and had picked out the nicest moss-covered red rocks to build it with. I brought back, also, wild ferns and trailing flowering vines, to plant on each tier.

During sheep shearing time in June, my sister, with two of her girl friends from Santa Fe, came to visit me. One day Ven sent word to Juan, our sheep foreman, that we were coming up next morning. He sent Sofio, who was a good fisherman, ahead. By the time we reached camp at noon,

109

ROMANCE OF A LITTLE VILLAGE GIRL

Sofio was there with a long string of mountain trout. Juan had a fat lamb hanging under a tree, and the cook had a pot of beans boiling on the campfire and was baking the nicest fat *tortillas* in the dutch oven buried in the coals. What a grand meal we had of fried trout, barbecued lamb, beans, tortillas and the best tasting coffee, although it was just cheap Arbuckle's. We had taken with us a box of biscuits and fruit tarts, but relished the camp cooking much more, especially after doing some mountain climbing and coming down with a ravishing appetite. The girls found it so much fun sleeping in tents and beds laid on the ground that they cried when we took them home.

Late that fall, I was again surrounding myself with all the beautiful things, flowers, lovely pictures, books — browsing over works of those who had lived noble, useful lives — trying in this manner to mold into a beautiful character the mind and disposition of the baby who would come to us in the spring.

In April, at the El Paso Hospital, a baby girl gladdened our hearts. This time the nurse, Miss Acuna, was most careful with my baby. She bathed the baby right there on her little crib in my room. She knew a baby must be kept warm.

The baby was a perfect blonde, with big, rare hazel blue eyes, taking after some of the Jaramillo's family; but only in looks, for my efforts had worked like a charm. My baby, Rosa Amelia, was as good as an angel. Nurse Vita, whom I brought from El Paso, marveled at the baby's goodness. The whole family adored her.

The bliss in which I was now living my happy existence would have been complete, as now my health was better and I felt stronger; however, when our baby reached the captivating age of fifteen months, and her sweet ways and tiny fingers had entwined in our heart strings, cholera infantum tore her out of our hearts, leaving us more sorrow-stricken than after the loss of our first baby. For eighteen days and nights I kept vigil by my sick baby's crib, looking up at a picture I had tacked by my bed. It was of a beautiful mother sitting

110

BACK AT THE COUNTRY HOME

by an old-fashioned crib, with one hand rocking her sick baby and her other arm resting by a lit candle on the table beside her, her eyes fastened on a picture of Christ compassionately looking down at her. Her lips were parted, repeating: "Jesus, Lover of our souls, have mercy on me." With tearful eyes I repeated the prayer over and over again. Sleeping powders had no effect on me. The picture is still by my bed, and I love it, although sad memories are connected with it.

Vita had loved our baby as if she had been her own; I did not have the heart to discharge her and kept her to do the cooking. She was slow, but very good at preparing the Mexican dishes which my husband enjoyed for a change. How could I now keep my resolution to stay at home at least during the summer? My house seemed so empty. As soon as Ven would say, "I am going to such a place; do you want to go?" I was ready.

While on one of these visits in Denver, ex-Governor Prince came to the Savoy Hotel with an invitation for us to attend a reception that Senator Walsh was giving out at Woolhurst, his country estate, in honor of Sen. and Mrs. Pinchot. Ven was out buying goods for our store. Knowing that he would not object to my going with a perfect old gentleman like the governor, I went, interested in meeting these noted people, whom I enjoyed. The receiving line stood outside the front of the simple, small building. Refreshments were served on a long table set out on the lawn under a long awning. The sitting room and dining room were opened for the guests. I was expecting to see a larger and more elaborate place, and was sort of disappointed at its simplicity.

CHAPTER XIX

Politics Are Fascinating

That fall, Ven went stronger into politics, and at the next two elections he won the office as senator from Rio Arriba County. During the first term of the legislature an interesting fight arose. The assembly created two new state institutions. Three senators came into the contest to carry one of them to their own home town. Ven came in for the reform school and won it. As one of the regents and treasurer, he directed the building of the first main building. Before the school opened, it was changed to the present Spanish-American Normal.

He worked hard for the school's improvement and growth. Today it has become a big institution of great help to all the inhabitants of the northern section of the state, and a monument to his memory.

Recently I sent an enlarged copy of his photograph to be hung in the new auditorium building.

The first year that Ven was in the senate the legislature had a very distinguished personnel. Among the members was Col. Francisco Chavez, president of the senate; Capt. Maximiliano Luna and Maj. Lewellyn, both members of the famous Rough Riders troop of the Spanish-American War; and Judge Albert Fall, who afterwards received so much publicity in the Teapot Dome Scandal while he was Secretary of the Interior. There were other bright attorneys

112

POLITICS ARE FASCINATING

who were members, good friends of my husband's who helped him get his bills passed.

It was interesting to go to the legislature to hear the heated arguments when there was a good debate. The moment a member rose to make a speech, Pedregon, the Spanish interpreter, rose at his side, filling in phrases in flowery Spanish, often making the best speech of the two. The legislature's wives were given reserved seats to the right of the speaker's chair.

At that time the old Palace Hotel, a frame building, was the only hotel in town and had poor accommodations; so most of the senators who had their wives with them stopped at the St. Vincent Sanitarium, which was then more of a guest house than a hospital, and a very nice play to stay.

After meals our group of ladies sat around the pleasant lobby chatting, the men joining us after dinner in the evening. But soon they found some excuse to leave, most often to attend a caucus at the Palace Hotel. These usually lasted until midnight, and some of the younger women who were trying to keep track of their husbands became worried. On one occasion when the wife of the senator from Carlsbad, called up her husband and told him he better be coming right away. The men thought they would play a joke on her. Two of the men took the senator by the arm between them, pulled his hat down over his face, and knocked at the wife's door. When she saw him in this apparently drunken condition, she grabbed him by the arm furiously, pulling his hat off. The husband straightened up, and the men left with a good laugh.

The society all called on the legislature ladies and extended invitations to teas and dinners. Party calls were then scrupulously returned on the lady's "day at home." On these days when callers were received, the tea table was already set by the fireplace, ready for tea to be served. One was sure to find one's friends in, especially as each side of town had its own appointed receiving days. The hostess usually invited some of her friends to bring their fancy work and

113

sit with her while waiting for the callers. The social life was formal and interesting in the capital.

The climax of entertainment was the formal evening reception at the Governor's Mansion. Governor and the first Mrs. Otero were very formal entertainers, and so were ex-Governor and Mrs. Prince. On one occasion two young ladies, editors on the staff of the *Chicago Journal,* were in town and some of the prominent people were showing them a good time, to give them a good impression of the old town. Governor and Mrs. Otero and Mr. and Mrs. Bergers invited them and us for a ride to the Tesuque Indian Pueblo. The Indian governor came out to meet us. Mr. Berger, introducing him, said: "Governor of New Mexico, meet the Governor of Tesuque." The Indian, very much pleased, invited us into his little two-room mansion. I had foolishly worn on the ride a short fur-trimmed velvet cape, and sitting in the front seat of the carriage I had been uncomfortably cold. I had not uttered a word; all I could do was to keep my teeth from chattering. A cup of wine served to us at the Bergers' on our return was a thankful treat.

That evening the young ladies, Ven and I were invited to Governor Prince's residence. In their long living room the governor had a collection of old, curious, silver-trimmed bridles, silver spurs and other things interesting to outsiders. Mrs. Prince picked up from a shelf a hideous-looking skull, and passed around showing it, telling us: "This is Montezuma's skull. Here is the dent where the stone hit that killed him." The first young woman drew away in disgust. The other one, most vivacious, took it between her arms and said: "Now I can say that I have hugged Montezuma's skull."

I very much enjoyed meeting intelligent people, but fresh from nine years of secluded convent life, in my timidity, I encased myself in a quiet reserve before an English-speaking gathering. Not having enough practice in speaking their language fluently, nor being yet schooled in their social ways, I was afraid to make a mistake, and rather profited by my quiet observation; although I felt I was giving people

114

the impression of being stupid, and many times felt dissatis-fied with myself because I was not a smarter woman, more able to help my husband more intelligently to carry on his social and political ambitions. Nevertheless, I never turned down an invitation that I thought I should accept, no matter how I preferred to have stayed quietly at home.

In compensation, I tried to make up for my wants by keeping scrupulously faithful to my home duties and making our home as attractive and comfortable as I could, for Ven and for his friends.

A year after, in the fall, a second baby girl had come to us. I was so disheartened by now that I had not tried to mold her either way, letting things be as they would. A delicate brunette she was, with her father's bright sparkle in her unusually big, black eyes, admired by every one. Nature endowed her with my family looks but with the Jaramillos' lively, volatile temperament, easily aroused, but generous, kind and affectionate like her father, who took after his mother's family, the Luceros and Gallegos. Born in October, the month dedicated to the Holy Angeles, Sister Angelica, at the hospital, insisted that she be given an angelic name. To please her, I added Angelina to Eloisa Biatriz, which I already had chosen to name her. Her extravagant father or-dered six dozen American Beauty roses for the christening; my room and the chapel at the hospital were like a fragrant garden. "What an extravagant man," Sister Mary Austin said, and next turned around and asked him for a donation to put in an elevator, which of course he handed out to her.

CHAPTER XX

The Territory Becomes a State

After decades of controversy between the two political parties — one favoring statehood, the other, territorial government — the statehood party won, and on January 6, 1912, President Howard Taft signed the proclamation of statehood in the presence of Congressman George Curry, and New Mexico became the forty-seventh star in the flag of the United States. A little later, one hundred elected members — my husband one of them — met at the capitol as members of the Constitutional Convention, to form the laws of the new state.

On January 15, Governor William McDonald, the first elected executive of New Mexico was inaugurated. On the eve of the inauguration, the governor and his family arrived from their Carrizoso ranch in a Santa Fe Railroad Pullman.

Elaborate preparations had been made. The dome of the capitol was illuminated with myriads of electric lights. At the entrance to the plaza blazed a welcoming arch. White and yellow bunting formed a background to the many rows of lights that lit the front of the Palace of the Governors; above glittered a star of lights and the name of Governor McDonald, together with the names of the first three governors, Oñate, De Vargas and Bent. The reception held in one of the large rooms in the Old Palace was a very formal affair, attended only by those holding tickets or invitations.

THE TERRITORY BECOMES A STATE

At the end, the governor and guests passed into the National Guard Armory, which had been decorated for the dance. Governor and Mrs. McDonald led the grand march, followed by Governor Mills, Lieutenant Governor E. de Baca, Adjutant General Brooks, Democratic Chairman C. C. Jones and Republican Chairman Ven Jaramillo, accompanied by their wives.

At eleven o'clock, dinner was served in the assembly room, which had been decorated, and set with small tables. Many costly gowns were seen on the guests. Silk marquisette was in style. Mrs. McDonald's gold satin one was veiled with black marquisette. I had ordered mine from the Denver Dry Goods Company, and it came in yellow marquisette with a dresden-flowered border in colors, outlined in black, with a yellow satin foundation. I still have it as a souvenir of the last great function I attended with my husband. He was still in the governor's staff and was in his full colonel's uniform.

That following summer our Denver girl friends paid us an unexpected visit. The Rev. McMenemin, rector of the Denver cathedral and an eloquent orator, was with them. They had been visiting my cousins named Burns at Tierra Amarilla, and on their way back to Denver, stopped at our house overnight.

At the dinner table Ven told the priest that I still remembered the first sermon I had heard him preach, when he had fired out: "We will build the Denver cathedral in spite of the people of Denver." "Yes," he said. "I first ask them to do something, then I plead. When that does not work, I scold." He built it, costing over one million dollars. Some people thought his sermons too flowery. For myself, I like variation, a change from the common, everyday expressions.

Next morning I joined the party to show them the way through Taos. The road through the Rio Grande canyon was steep and rough, but our reverend friend proved to be an expert driver, and we passed through Taos late in the afternoon. A little ways out of town a shower met us, and Father, not being used to the Taos sticky mud, stopped to put on chains. In the meantime I sat in the car, enraptured, watching the undescribable panorama as the shower played on the beautiful Taos Mountains. A misty white fog was rising from the foot of the mountains. The top peaks were shrouded in dark clouds, now and then lit up by zigzag lightning. Shafts of golden sun rays shot from behind dark clouds and hit green spots on the mountains, and here and there around the valley sheets of rain poured down.

In about an hour we reached Arroyo Hondo. At my old home my three brothers were batching; but they had a good cook, and our flourishing appetites soon were quenched with the simple but nourishing menu served. The girls' father owned a cattle ranch; so they knew something about ranch life, and enjoyed the visit. Because of the lack of wine and hosts, the priest could not give us mass next morning in our private chapel before leaving.

> "Let the old houses their secrets keep
> Leave them alone in their quiet sleep;
> They are like old folks who nod by the fire,
> Glad with their dreams of youth and desire."

My next trip to Taos was with my friend, Ruth Laughlin Barker, author of the popular book, *Caballeros*. She wanted to see an old Spanish-style house to describe in her new book. On the way, I described some of the big, attractive homes I knew when I was in school at Taos. It was during the rainy month of April, and a little shower met us as we were coming into town. Next morning, when I raised the window shade in my room at the Don Fernando Hotel, another enchanting sight met my eyes. Down in the valley, the peach and apricot trees covered with pink and white blossoms, and above, the high, snow-clad mountains blinded the eyes with their brilliancy in the brightest sunshine. No wonder Taos valley has always since my childhood fascinated me like a fairyland.

118

THE TERRITORY BECOMES A STATE

After breakfast, we rode to Ranchito, but where was Aunt Piedad's attractive old home, or the new one grandpa had built for her? It was hard to believe my eyes that what I was seeing were the melting remains of these once big, fine lively homes. A sob choked in my throat.

After lunch, I thought of the Valdez home at Placita. The round *torrion* always had marked this nice home for me; but now I could not find it; and we rode on to Arroyo Seco to see the fine Gonzales home. We were standing right before it, but I did not recognize it. "Where is Juanita Gonzales' home?" I asked a man in the yard. "This is the house." he answered. The whitewashed porch with the blue railing posts was gone, and the whole house was in ruins. Juanita, whom her mother always had kept so well-dressed at school, came to the door with torn hose and shabby shoes. She asked us to come in. I asked her if she had some of her mother's fine jewelry or table silver. She brought out a silver set with an exquisite design and silver grape bunches on the lids. My friend became interested right away to buy it. Juanita asked $35.00. I am sure it was worth more, but my friend continued to bargain until finally she said, "I will give you a $15.00 check." I shook my hand at the side "no," but Juanita only smiled at me, showing her pretty dimples, and answered, "Alright." This is how our rich Spanish families have been stripped of their most precious belongings. "Why did you do it?" I whispered as I was going out the door. "I need the money to fix the house," she said.

At the Don Fernando (once the Barron Hotel), Mr. Gusdorf, the proprietor, kept introducing me to the hotel guests, telling them I had been married in this hotel. Oh, how I wished the old hotel had been as fine and attractive as this new one, to accommodate our wedding guests.

119

CHAPTER XXI

My Father Retires From Business

My father now retired from business in Taos County and moved his family to Santa Fe, leaving my three oldest brothers to manage the store, farms and stock.

In Santa Fe, my father bought from Mr. Arthur Stabb the land running from what is now McKenzie Street to the Arroyo Mascaras. He divided it into lots and built the first three brick houses on the east side of Chapelle Street. The family occupied one of these, and the others were rented.

The government had, a few years before, removed the military militia from the city, and now it donated the Fort Marcy addition to the city school board. The board threw the property open for sale, and my father bought one of the officers' houses on Grant Street, renovated it, and moved the family into this more desirable location.

The town was very quiet after the militia left. "We miss the gay militia dances," Doña Candelaria said to my mother, telling her how she loved to dance with *"los del guante blanco,"* the white-gloved officers, and the jealous quarrels the Padre Gallegos, her husband, had with her after the dances.

This Padre Gallegos had forsaken his church, married Candelaria, entered politics, and was elected delegate to the U. S. Congress.

Felipita, a niece whom Candelaria had adopted, also became entangled in trouble when the young American, Tip-

120

ton, became very attentive to her and finally took courage one evening to go to her home to propose to her. The Padre objected, saying that in the first place Tipton was a foreigner, and in the second place he had no dowry to offer.

The poor girl was locked up in one of the back bedrooms and only allowed to go out when chaperoned by her aunt. Nevertheless the lover continued to court his sweetheart through the latticed back window, and by notes sent to her through her maid. One evening the maid helped her mistress elope. The couple was married at Guadalupe church and returned to ask forgiveness, which of course the parents refused to grant.

Several years later young Tipton proved to be a bright young man. He mastered the Spanish language and was sent to Spain to translate Spanish archives. Later he was sent as an envoy to the Philippine Islands.

Too steady mental work and too many hard, cold political campaign trips and poor accommodations out in country villages contributed to break down Ven's health, never too good. He underwent an operation at the Battle Creek Sanitarium and returned home with renewed cheerfulness, feeling that he had been cured. But in a few years his malady returned, and he again went to the same sanitarium for treatments. This time he took Angelina and me with him.

After I had gone through my tests I received an invitation from Dr. Kellog to come to his office that evening and bring with me my husband and daughter. I presume that the history of my tests had been sent in to him and he was curious to see if we were a family of midgets. Two other women had also been called to his office perhaps for him to find out if they were giants. One weighed three hundred, the other, five hundred pounds. One morning while going through our mechanical exercises, when my turn came to sit in the double electric chair, the monstrous woman was already sitting on one side and then I took the other. The line of women going through other exercises had to stop and laugh at the curious sight we must have made. I wondered which of the two was funnier.

On one of his trips east, Ven came back in a new Stutz car. Automobiles were still such a rare sight in our village that people gathered around it to examine it. On our first trip to Santa Fe in this car Ven sent Gabriel early in the morning with the team of horses, telling him to wait for us at the Chama River crossing at Abiquiu. When old Rosalia saw us passing through the village in the car, she stood at the door crossing herself and imploring her Lady of Guadalupe to protect us. She thought this horseless car must be run by some evil spirit, not understanding how it could run without horses. After the team pulled the car across the Chama River, Ven, thinking we were now on safe road, sent the team back. Soon the car sank into a mudhole in an irrigation ditch. With aid of fence poles our chauffeur, Segura, finally lifted the car out. A few miles further the car sank deep in the sandy Arroyo del Toro. We sat patiently waiting for help and along came "Juan Borullas," who did more talking than work. He tied his long rope to the car and then to his horse's saddle and pulled the car out. From there on our progress was still slow but more pleasant, especially when we came into the Chama River valley and saw it covered with a mantle of autumn coloring. The little adobe houses were festooned with freshly-strung bright red chile peppers. By evening, we reached Santa Fe.

I was so tired from the hard jolting that I was disgusted with the fine car. Those first red cars had hard springs, and I had to hold on fast to the sides to keep from bouncing up and hitting my head on the top. I had come home with a black eye from another ride, and Ven had made poor Segura accountable for trying to speed. I felt safer riding in my rubber-tired phaeton. My plunging white horse only accelerated his speed when shying at a honking car. My progressive husband, however, enjoyed taking relatives and friends on their first automobile ride. The streets in town were not much better than our rough country roads. I have a Kodak picture of one of these rides, my dear friend,

122

MY FATHER RETIRES FROM BUSINESS

Mrs. Diaz, at the wheel. The chauffeur took the picture. I am seen with my hat tied with one of those large veils that we wore to hold our hats in the strong wind in the half-open cars, which were cold and uncomfortable.

The health of my family grew more delicate, and we decided to build a winter home in Santa Fe, where we could have more of the modern comforts. The bungalow-style houses had hit the city and the six-room-house I planned was built in this style. It had all the conveniences that save time and work. By November we were enjoying our new home with its fine furnishings. My husband's Christmas present to me was a three-hundred-dollar, diamond-disc phonograph, with a dozen fine opera records. We spent a very comfortable winter, and in the spring went back to our country home. There we went through the usual busy summer.

In the fall, Ven had a severe attack of illness. He had suffered all night quietly till morning. When he heard Sofio coming up the walk, he called to him and told him to hitch the buggy and go to Espanola and bring Dr. Brook. That night the doctor brought Ven into town. Next morning, I followed by train with my baby, Angie, and Vivi, her fat nurse.

In a few days Ven recovered enough to make the trip to Denver. With infinite patience he tried to hide his suffering, never mentioning his ills. By spring he felt better, and we returned home to attend to his business. I marveled at his strong willpower, at his inexhaustible energy and his intelligent qualities with which nature had enriched him as a recompense for his frail constitution. Ardent in all his feelings towards his family, he rendered for us the deep well of affection that swelled in his heart, showering on all his family his care and generosity. He was always helping people to better their condition in life, by giving or lending them the means they needed to start in business. As busy a man as he was, when on his business trips to the city, he always found time to attend to errands for his village people. Gifts

123

that he brought me left a lifetime memory of his unfailing love and thoughtfulness. He never returned without bringing me a gift, a fine picture, or motto, a set of fine dishes, a jewel or piece of furniture, until the house was so full that I had to ask him to please not bring another thing. "Well," he said, "if I bring you a hat or a dress I know it won't be what you like. If I bring you a box of candy, you keep it until it gets stale." It was true; I waited until I had company to help me eat the rich candy.

As to clothes, no one could ever please my fastidious taste in that. He had made for me a fine beaver fur coat, from beavers caught at our Chama ranch. I wore it a few times to please him, but oh, the weight! It seemed like he could never go into a store without seeing something nice to buy for me. Once while on a trip buying bucks in Utah, he became confused about the date of our wedding anniversary and set me a beautiful diamond-set platinum locket. I found when I went to Denver that these lockets and chains were the latest jewelry fad. Another time while delivering lambs in Denver, he treated Juan, one of his sheepherders, to the trip. Showing him the city, Ven took him into the Denver Dry Goods Store. Trying to find a set of furs that would be the right size for me, Ven asked two or three of the girl clerks to try on several sets. Collarettes came to the knees then, and the muffs covered me out of sight. Ven picked out the smallest set, paid for it and left.

He took Juan into a movie, something new to Juan. When Juan saw in the picture a monster train engine speeding close up to them, he jumped out of his seat ready to run. Ven, laughing, pulled him back by his coat tail, asking "What is the matter with you?" "*Por Dios!* I thought we were going to get killed," Juan answered, still scared. Ven enjoyed taking his country friends to the city and playing innocent jokes on them. On another occassion he ordered a dish of frog legs for the friend he had with him at dinner. "How did you like that dish?" Ven asked Don Jose. "Boy! these chicken legs were good," Don Jose answered. He was furious when Ven told him they were frog legs.

MY FATHER RETIRES FROM BUSINESS

Realizing that his health would no longer permit him to be away from his doctor, Ven sold his mercantile store at El Rito and we went to spend the winter in Denver. He bought an apartment house and nine building lots, expecting to be able to sell his sheep and ranch and transfer his business to that city.

Each year of suffering added to his countenance deeper lines, but he disguised all with apparent cheerfulness. In my anxious solicitude I could guess the inner torments beneath his touching efforts to appear well, and I admired his noble spirit of endurance of suffering.

Still refusing to be an invalid he went to Johns Hopkins Hospital. The radium treatment did not seem to help him. On his return to Denver, he found a client interested in buying the sheep and sheep ranch. Ven left with him to show him the sheep at the Navajo reservation, where the sheep wintered. The spring weather was rainy and cold, and he returned looking much worse. "Did you make a sale?" I asked him. "No, the man offered only eleven dollars a head for the sheep and three-fifty an acre for the land." "I remember when you used to sell old ewes for four dollars. Now just because prices are high you still want more," I told him. "Oh well, these prices are good for two years more," he said.

That fall Juan, his sheep *caporal,* came in to report before we left for Denver. I heard Ven say to him: "This ranch has made me sweat." At the supper table I asked him: "How are you coming with the ranch?" "We are coming out alright," he answered, never wanting me to know about his worries. "Why did you buy such a big world? We don't have so many sheep," I had said when he bought the ranch. "Because we Mexicans can only make money with sheep, and land is getting scarce."

While Ven was away I had packed the furniture and our clothes, expecting to leave for home as soon as he returned. Instead we moved to the Argonaut Hotel. Not giving up yet his search for health, it occurred to him that the mineral waters at Ojo Caliente, near our home, had always helped

125

him; we left for Idaho Springs. I found him one day with a very sad expression on his face, holding a telegram in his hand. It read: "I am pleased to congratulate you on your election as a delegate to the national convention and extend to you the hospitality of the Leonard Wood headquarters, Congress Hotel." His friends are still showering honors on him which his failing health prevented him from accepting. I laid the telegram on the table without finding a word to say; I felt what he was thinking.

In a week I noticed the swift change coming on him. He had grown so weak he could hardly walk to the dining room. His cheerfulness had now changed to a sad expression. I suggested going back to Denver and for him to go to a hospital, where he could receive better care. On the train, as I sat by him, he touched my hand. "You are warm," he said. His hands were cold. "Yes, those mineral waters are heating to me," I said, touched by his sad tone and look, especially when little Angie came near him.

CHAPTER XXII

Suns Go Down

"Life has its spring —
The rosy years of youth,
Its summer of achievement;
Then autumn with its piece
of work well done,
Brings rest and understanding
of the whole.

Then winter's long night sets in,
When autumn's sunset colors fade away,
Like embers on the hearthstone
burning low;
The soul must rest,
Her weary eyelids close."

Early one morning in the latter part of May, I was aroused from my sleep by a telephone call saying to come to St. Anthony's Hospital. For two days and three nights I sat by the bedside of my very ill husband. Numb with grief, I held his hand tight, as if in this way I could stay his going. It seemed impossible that we could part. I only left his side when I felt as if I would drop down in a faint.

To the last day he tried to show his deep affection. With his eyes closed, unable to open them any more, he stretched his hand, caressingly touching my face. How I wanted to

127

lay my head on the pillow close to his and tell him how I loved him, for beneath my exterior reserve there had always burned the most ardent love which my reserve kept me from showing. Across the bed sat my kind friend, Mrs. Dornis, a lady I had met at the Argonaut Hotel. She meant well, and kept vigil with me all day and part of the night. Other friends kept coming in and out, quietly, but oh, how I wished to be left alone with my dear one in his last hours. The nurse sitting by me, running her fingers over the veins on my hands that were standing out like thick cords from the strain on my emotions, said to me: "You had better take a rest." But no sooner would I throw myself down on the cot in the next room than Mrs. Dornis would be at the door calling me back. "He must see you there if he opens his eyes," she would say.

At three o'clock in the morning on the thirtieth of May the crushing blow fell. I still held his hand tightly, kneeling by his bed. As the cord of his life broke, I felt something rush into my hand. Was this undescribable thing something of my husband's spirit that passed into me, through my hand? Was this what gave me the courage and strength needed? Something appeared to be holding me up and leading me. It seemed to say: "Your baby needs you, and there is work for you. Brace up."

Alone in a strange city with only a few friends around me, I felt that I must fight this crushing grief in my heart and face whatever came my way. I kept up my courage and attended to the funeral arrangements, even to selecting the casket and cemetery plot. It was only when the clerk at the store draped the black mourning veil over my face that every drop of blood seemed to leave me. I held on to the chair as my strength gave away. My sincere friend, Marie, was with me all through my trouble, and now went with me to see the Rev. McMenemin about the church services. Bishop Pitaval, once fiery preacher at the Santa Fe cathedral and now retired and acting chaplain at St. Anthony's Hospital, visited and comforted my husband all through his illness and officiated at the high funeral mass in the cathedral.

SUNS GO DOWN

The Rev. McMenemin gave a very touching eulogy, mentioning how my little girl looking up to heaven the night before had said: Mother, that bright star up there is my papa."

It was the day after Decoration Day when my beloved husband's remains were laid at rest in Mount Olivet Cemetery. The whole cemetery seemed to have been decorated for his funeral. The weather was damp and cool, and the flowers covering the green plots were still fresh.

This relieved some of that depressing sadness that would have accompanied his funeral had it taken place in that neglected graveyard at El Rito. My first baby's remains I now had moved from my friend Marie's plot and buried by his father. The relatives and friends living in Denver and my sister and her husband were the only ones who attended the funeral. Those living in New Mexico were deeply disappointed. They were expecting to attend it there at home.

With a heavy heart I returned to my parent's home in Santa Fe. As soon as Ven's attorney, Judge Wright, and Mr. Mardorf, president of the C. C. Bank, learned that I was in town, they called to ask me for my husband's last will. They knew he had executed one before leaving for Denver. I knew nothing about it. Ven, seeing how worried I already was about his illness, had kept from telling me of it. The men advised me to go home and look for it and bring it together with any other important papers I might find. Taking with me my little girl I went to the country home we had so loved. We found it now so empty and lonely. How we missed the life that had been enriched with love and comfort. In vain I listened for the familiar step on the sidewalk, for the warm, "Hello, *mi vida!*" — that re-echoed through the hall as we met at the door and arm in arm walked through the house, then to the dining room to sit at an attractively set table replenished with a well-prepared meal that Ven would be sure to praise. Once my mother heard him and said to me, "It must be a pleasure to cook for a man like Ven." Yes, it was; it turned drudgery into a pleasure.

129

ROMANCE OF A LITTLE VILLAGE GIRL

The people of the village who had so esteemed and respected my husband, hearing that I had come home, came to offer their sympathy. Expressing their great grief, they mingled their tears with mine, saying: "A big man has passed away, one who contributed much to our comfort and happiness." Yes, a big man had disappeared from the political and social scene of northern New Mexico, and for me the happiest epoch of my life had ended. An irreparable loss it was, not only to his family, his mother and sisters he had taken care of, but also to his whole community. He had felt it his duty to share in the duties of government and justice and saw that the laws were enforced and respected. During his life the people had lived in peace and harmony, but a few years after he departed this life, plunder, burning of buildings and murder disturbed the peace that had reigned before. The law became so lenient that the culprits sentenced to punishment were in a few years set free through political influence. The law-abiding citizens now lived in fear of their safety, too timid to make any complaint.

For two weeks, between receiving callers, I searched through packed desk drawers and paper files. Ven had carried on his business very systematically, and always left a copy of his answer pinned to all important letters. Every day I read piles of papers until my eyes hurt. Each day I found out more about how involved in debt his estate was, and felt more grieved and humiliated. His business had been somewhat neglected the past few years on account of his illness, which forced him to be absent from it. In the process of being transferred to Denver, it had become in a very bad shape. The heavy interest charges on money borrowed to pay for the sheep ranch at Chama had each year eaten up the profits made by the sheep. He had assumed a mortgage on the apartment building he bought in Denver and the past-due taxes on the nine lots. The cattle ranch he willed to his mother. The only properties left free of debt were the two homes and two farms at El Rito. I found the will, and although he knew my extreme timidity and my ignorance about estate matters and court proceeding, Ven had shown his confidence in me by naming me executrix of his estate, together with my father. Gathering the will, property deeds, the inventory list I wrote out of all the properties and everything I thought of importance, I took them to Judge Wright in Santa Fe. With his great experience in estate matters he foresaw trouble ahead and asked me if I did not have something in my own name. "Just a herd of sheep my father had given me," I told him. The house I had on Lincoln Avenue I had sold to the Art Museum board. Ven had borrowed the money from me and had never paid it back. The attorney advised me to put in a claim for the money against the estate. I sent my father to the courthouse, where he found the deed registered in my name. With this evidence I placed my claim. The probating of the will settled, I returned home to see that faithful Sofio who had been our farmhand for over nine years, and who still stood by me in my hour of need, would hire the help to harvest the hay, wheat and oats he had planted that spring.

To add to my already heavy worries, I received the bank statement of my personal account marked, "Overdrawn." The president of the bank had credited the little cash I had in my name, to the interest on estate notes that Ven owed. I was holding the statement in my hand when little Angie looking up from where she was sitting, playing with her blocks. She must have noticed my tearful eyes. She got up and came and put her arms around me, saying: "I wish I had died instead of little brother." "Why?" I asked. "Because he would be bigger and could help you," she answered. "You are helping me more by staying here with me. Little brother would be out playing with the boys." Many times before I had been surprised by the thoughtfulness of this four-year-old child.

Grieved beyond words, I did not let anyone know about this bank affair. I thought it was my duty to help pay my husband's debts. People did not seem to understand that his life had been cut off before he had completed his task. We managed to get along by selling some of my personal things

131

and Angie's nursery furniture, which she no longer needed.

A notice came from the railroad agent at Barranca Station, saying that a carload of farm machinery was there addressed to Ven. The bill offered a ten percent discount if paid in thirty days. There was no time to lose. I sent the teams to the station to haul this freight, and sent Sofio to the post office to get me a dozen penny post cards and told him to stop at the store and find out at what price these farm machines were sold there.

I immediately addressed the cards to farmers who lived in the near villages, giving them a list of the farm machines and setting the price five dollars cheaper than the price charged at the store. I not only sold the new ones, but also sold all the old discarded ones under the shed, and harnesses and other old junk filling the storerooms. I cleared for the estate three thousand dollars, adding the cash from the crops Sofio harvested that fall.

This work finished, I wrote to Ven's relative who had been runing the apartment house in Denver to tell her that I would be there by October 1 to take charge of the apartment. This was a great shock to her, as she had thought she could claim the property. She had told her friends that I did not know anything about business, and she, the business woman of the family, was going to run things to her liking. It was true — I had never managed any business; but I had never set myself to learn anything that I did not learn, and necessity is the best teacher.

For two weeks she refused to give up the house, and I with my baby put up living in a dingy little room upstairs. I had gone to her door one evening to try and explain how matters stood, but she furiously closed the door in my face. Finally, not able to prove her claim, she vacated.

Something was guiding me. I found the book in which Ven had written the salary he was paying her, the price he had paid for the property and the name of the firm of attorneys who had handled the deal for him. I took the book to these lawyers and told them my troubles.

Out of the nine thousand dollars yearly rents, I found

only three hundred cash left in the apartment bank account, and a large plumbing bill to be paid. In a month I had cleared the bills and had the plumbing, which was in very bad condition, fixed, in spite of the big bill. From then on I cut down by half all running expenses. In three months I had saved and paid on the mortgage two thousand dollars, and wrote to the estate attorney advising him of this. He was out of town and my letter was handed to the bank president, who wrote to tell me not to make any more payments on that property, that all the estate money had to be handled through his bank. I was disappointed, for I had figured I could pay off the mortgage in less than three years. Later the attorney wrote to me to try and sell the property. I answered that I did not think this would be wise, as this was the only income-paying property left to the estate. The sheep had been sold for half the price that had been offered to Ven. The man who had the sheep ranch rented, credited the very low rent to the interest on the mortgage he held on the ranch. Renters on the El Rito farms owed most of the rent.

I held on to the apartment house for a year. In September, Jones, the janitor, came and told me that the back hall door would not stay open. I had noticed down in the basement a wide crack on the north wall, and figured that the building was settling to that side. If the wall collapsed, it would take the six thousand dollars I had now saved from the rents to build it. I had the door fixed. Very much worried, I went to see Mr. Dornis at the Argonaut Hotel and listed with him the apartment house for sale. Ten days later Mr. Dornis brought me a buyer. I gave them an option at several thousand dollars below cost. That was a worried, sleepless night. In the morning I went to my friends, the Spencers, and told them of the terrible thing I had done. "Why, my dear lady, that is all the property is worth, and you must also figure the rents you have made," good George told me. I went back to my room feeling relieved, figuring also that rents had started going down. The depression after World War I had started to hit the country. In a few days

133

the deal was closed, and with regret I handed over the property deed to the buyer. I wrote to the estate attorney to tell him of the sale. When I appeared before the Denver probate court judge to hand in my final report, he had already heard from the attorney in Santa Fe to the effect that the estate in New Mexico might become insolvent and to do what he could for me. The kind judge said to me: "I am always for the widow."

My furniture and other things all packed, I bade goodbye to my Denver friends. They had all been so kind, especially to my little orphan, taking her on rides and to their homes. One friend said to me: "I am glad you are going back to your folks. I was afraid you would not pull through this year." It had been a hard year, with my spirits so depressed, my baby catching every ill that came along, and the estate in such a muddle.

I felt but a sad relief when I opened my Santa Fe home again and rented to artist Rollins and his wife the front bedroom, as I did not like being alone. With hopes of selling the Chama ranch I applied every spare minute I had to advertising it for sale, drawing maps and answering ads and inquiries.

Ven's relatives had not come near us in Denver. Hearing that I was back in my home, the mother wrote asking if she could come and stay with us that winter. I answered that my health was so bad I could hardly keep up to attending to my work. For five years I had been putting off a badly-needed operation, waiting for my little daughter to be older and more able to attend to herself. It could not be put off any longer. I appointed guardians for her, wrote my last will and went to the hospital with little hope of coming out alive. Little Angie, not having any money to buy me florist's flowers, fixed up a little basket with crepe paper and filled it with pansies from our own garden and took it to me. The love, that I felt was enfolded in this poor little gift, touched my heart. I knew she felt bad about not bringing me something nicer, and I tried to make her feel my great appreciation of her thought.

My life was still to be spared longer, and in two weeks I was back at my mother's house. By spring I was able to go out to our country home and attend to renting the farms. One evening a heavy-set, red-haired cattleman came to the door inquiring about the Chama ranch. I asked him to come in and gave him a description of the land and price, but still he sat, asking me if I would rent him a room. I said no, that I did not rent rooms. He walked behind me, where I sat at my desk, and looked into my bedroom. "This is a nice room," he said. My heart beat faster. Showing a calm exterior I stood up behind my chair. He looked at me, smiling. Just then footsteps were heard on the sidewalk. The man walked to the door and stepped out on the porch. I followed him, concealing my fear. Here came Angie running up to me. I put my arms around her. "What a quiet place this is. Does the caretaker live in that house?" the man asked, pointing to the house we had for the hired help outside the garden. I should have said "yes," but I have always been too slow to invent a lie. "No, he lives up town," I answered. He walked down to the gate slowly taking a look all around. With my arm still around my little savior, I rushed her into the house and locked the door, sat at my desk and wrote a note to my neighbor, Mrs. Martin, asking her if she would please send one of her boys up town to ask Aurelia, the girl who came to work for me each morning to come and sleep with us that night. The girl was sick, but good Mrs. Martin sent two of her boys to sleep at my house for a couple of nights.

That was the first time I had brushed against an unpleasant situation. It warned me of the danger of being alone. I decided to pack everything and closed the house. With the aid of Sofio and Aurelia, in two weeks I had the furniture packed. Angie had parted with her play tent, lawn swing and the hammock which we had enjoyed so much, resting under the trees and looking up at the blue sky, listening to the rustling of the trees, swayed by the gentle breeze, and inhaling the sweet perfume of roses and flowers that the wind carried even into the house.

With a sad look back at the house, we left one morning, a truck full of the furniture I had not sold rolling behind us.

I had rented the bungalow before going out to the country, so we stayed at my mother's house on our return.

An offer came for the nine Denver lots. As the depression was still on, I had to sell them at below cost and pay the back taxes out of the sale cash. With the balance, and some cash left from the apartment house sale, I wanted to make another dividend payment to the estate creditors. But the attorney advised me to wait, saying the past taxes on the Chama ranch might have to be paid with this money. In the meantime several banks went into bankruptcy, and my bank among them. The estate money was lost. Each day matters became worse. I was now offering the sheep ranch at half price, but still buyers could not pay even this, as most of the cattle and sheep men had lost considerably during the last few years. I was offered some good properties in trade in California and Kansas, but was not allowed to accept them. Six thousand dollars in oil stock and two thousand in Read Products Company were a complete loss. Even my poor little Angie lost a little savings account I had started for her, and my father lost almost all he had in the closing of two banks.

The estate attorney, foreseeing that the ranch property might also be lost, had advised me to see an attorney and put in a claim for the cash I had loaned Ven, to be paid to me as a preferred claim. I asked Judge Roberts to attend to this for me, as he was of the same political party as Ven. I thought he and the estate attorney might work together in my behalf. By now I had courage to face almost anything. Accompanied by my father I sat in the court room listening to the interesting arguments of the lawers, The Albuquerque bank had sent two lawyers to contest my claim. One of the two was ex-governor Mechem, who had been my husband's good friend.

This was a trial that I had not yet experienced. Feeling

a bit shaky, I took the witness chair when I was called. I produced the only proof I had, the bank statement that showed where the cash I had in my personal account had been credited on estate notes. Judge Wright arose and said he had never heard of this before. True, I had not told him about it; most of my troubles I kept to myself. Judge Mechem said I had been taken advantage of by the bank president, and made no objection; but the other attorney strongly objected. The court had to rule that my claim should be paid at the same as the others, as a dividend payment.

Still I had hopes of selling the ranch and clearing all the debts. I had real-estate agents working on it all through the West. A Texas man who seemed very much interested in buying wired me that he could not come until after June 15, as he had been called East on important business. I wrote to ask the mortgage holder to extend me the time, two weeks, to pay off the small loan on the ranch, until this buyer came. He refused and foreclosed the mortgage. I just could not believe he would have ever done this. He is a wealthy man now. When his family came to our village, Ven helped them get started in business by having his grandmother lend them the money to buy the Grant store and home. I wonder if now that he has sold our tract of land for two hundred thousand dollars, if his conscience does not prick him for having appropriated it all and left all the other creditors out in the depression.

My last thread of hope in saving a home for my daughter broke, after nine years of hard work trying to save something.

By now my daughter had grown into a young lady, reserved but pleasure-loving. An ambitious student from the first grade up, she always had made the highest average in her class. My great disappointment was not being able to give her the advantages of the fine schooling her father would have wanted her to have, and to keep for her the country home which she dearly loved. Like a true country child,

137

ROMANCE OF A LITTLE VILLAGE GIRL

Angie was hypnotized by the sunny glitter and purple mystery of those distant mountains seen from our front porch — the only place I have ever seen a complete rainbow. After those summer thunderstorms, the vivid colors would circle over the dark sky across the valley from the foot of the hills in the east to the foot of the hills on the southwest, holding us in ecstasy. Horseback rides up the beautiful canyon, and picnics at the towering red bluffs were Angie's delights. She admired the expert horsemanship of the country boys and their simple tastes and happy lives.

She told me of a little incident she had witnessed while resting by the canyon river. "Down the road came a boy racing on his horse. He rode behind a tall bush and waited. Here came another boy riding one of those well-fed, shiny horses. Leisurely singing, he sat sideways on his saddle, the reins carelessly loose over the saddle horn. His song was suddenly interrupted by a loud yell from the other boy, who sprang out on the road, scaring the rider's horse. You ought to have seen how quickly that boy threw his leg over the saddle and grabbed the rein, but the scared horse raced some distance before the boy could stop it and turn back to meet the other boy. Both were laughing at the joke," she said. By the thrill in her voice I was able to visualize the scene and to feel her admiration and enjoyment. I longed to find ourselves again at those evening suppers by the river. Angie never outgrew her love of wading in the river and climbing hills. Her grief was having to part with the country home. "If you sell it, I am going to work until I earn enough money with which to buy it back. I have a lovely plan of having a big party with dancing in the big hall, the orchestra playing up on the balcony, and refreshments served in the open dining room," she would tell me. I kept this in my mind, and during the following summer vacation I invited my sister and her family and two of Angie's friends to visit us out at the country home. I took in my brother's car a load of bedding and groceries, and my sister took another load. Annette had gone ahead and found a maid for us, and with borrowed furniture and some of her own, had fixed up part of the house.

At the end of our visit it occurred to me that this was the last opportunity to have Angie's dream party. In a hurry I sent by messenger invitations to some of the nice girls and boys in town. I rode down to the lower village to invite the blind boy to come and play for the dance. The girls brought from the river green branches and vines, and decorated the dining room and living room and built a fire in the fireplace. My sister helped prepare the refreshments. Some of the girls to whom invitations were sent were out of town, and our neighbors, having some dislike for one of the boys invited, refused to come. This was a great disappointment. The blind man and his wife were the most eager to attend, and with their wee baby arrived too early. They enjoyed the refreshments more than anyone else, and left most happy. It was a small party. However, I was glad to have tried to grant Angie's wish, although it was not in the elaborate way she had dreamed it.

The day I closed the house, Angie's eyes shone brighter, full of tears, as we stood on the front porch filling our eyes with the beloved vista. I pretended not to notice, for my heart felt heavy, too, at this last farewell.

For we loved the mountains, the piñon tree-covered hills, the green fields, the wild flower-bordered aceqias, the wooded river and the warm little adobe homes. But most of all we loved our own.

How much fun we had every summer at this dear home, trying to do without maid help, with only good Sofio bringing in wood for the kitchen range — as neither of us had much strength, even to draw a bucket of water out of the well. We both hung on to the rope and pulled to bring it up. Then we stood by, laughing at our own helplessness. We rested and filled our lungs with that fresh pure air, and admired the lights and shadows that the newly-risen sun was spreading over mountains, hills and green fields.

My poor girl's life seemed mapped out for sacrifice. She had to give up the things she was most fond of, on account

139

of her frail constitution. Basketball was too strenuous for her. At track practice she fell and dislocated her knee. Horseback riding gave her hayfever. Music and reading were a great strain on her eyes; she now had to wear stronger lenses; but those two she would never give up. She grew up with a bookcase full of books, and even before she learned how to read she already knew so well the stories by heart and was so familiar with the words that she turned the pages exactly on the last word without a mistake.

Just about at the close of the school that summer, her dearest school friend, Margaret, passed away. "I just cannot stand to see Margaret's empty seat right in front of me," Angie said, with that sad resignation that was touching. "You don't have to go to Loretto this coming year. You can go to the academy in Albuquerque," I told her to console her.

That summer we were staying at a friend's house at El Rito while attending to some repairs at our house. A kind neighbor, who felt sorry for a young boy whose mother had divorced his father, and thought lively Angie would cheer him up, came and took her to introduce Angie to him. The result was the beginning of more than just a friendship. The boy's father was the contractor who was building the new gymnasium at the A. A. N. school, for which Senator Cutting had donated several thousands of dollars. This New York millionaire came out to New Mexico's healing sunshine in search of health. He built a nice home in Santa Fe, entered politics and revolutionized the Repulican party by starting an independent party. His political career was cut short by his tragic death while on one of his airplane trips between Santa Fe and his home city.

The young boy's interest in my daughter continued. On weekends when he came to town with his father he would call to see Angie. When they were leaving for Denver, he came and stayed until his father called him. From Denver he wrote sending his picture and asking for hers. "No," I said, "you do not want your picture flying around the country in the hands of a boy we know nothing about, except

140

that his mother left his father." This divorce gave me a doubtful opinion, and an excuse to object to her keeping up their correspondence. While Angie was at school I saw the boy's picture on her dresser. I put it away, replacing it with one of her Cousin Le Roy. She of course noticed the change when she went into her room after school. She came back crying with rage. "Yes, just because he is a poor boy you don't like him," she fired. No, it was not as she said. In my opinion, character, education and refinement have always counted more than money.

In a few days the storm blew away, but we were not the same. Angie grew cooler. I missed her kiss on her leaving for school and on going to bed. Too proud to apologize, I pretended to take it indifferently, saying, "Kisses have germs, they say."

By the end of school she had cheered up, being busy then with exams and the excitement of the coming junior-senior banquet. I sent her to bring me something from my old trunk that I had at my father's house. She came back delighted, holding up an old pink-embroidered chiffon skirt. "Look, Mumsy, you can make me a dress out of this and don't have to buy me a new one until next year for my graduation." "How considerate. I will try," I said. I went up town and bought a dress pattern for a very simple formal gown, long-waisted, with a full circular skirt. I found in my trunk a yard of pink chiffon to match, and set to cutting the dress, with inserts of plain chiffon to give fullness to the skirt. A picot-edged shawl collar was the only trimming. For a week I nearly broke my back sewing the dress all by hand. But the happy smile that lit Angie's face when she saw it on the hanger compensated for all my work. "Now go to my trunk and bring a wide, three-yard-long black velvet sash, that I used to wear with my nicest gowns," I said. She brought it. Her friends admiring the gown would ask, "And where did you get the velvet ribbon sash?" "All I have to do is go to mother's old trunk to find all kinds of nice things," Angie told them.

141

ROMANCE OF A LITTLE VILLAGE GIRL

It is a happy event when gay feasts come to wipe out of our hearts and minds some of our troubles. This happens on the first week in September, when Santa Fe celebrates its reconquest by Gen. De Vargas. How can young hearts resist the fun of dressing up in colorful costume, or resist the music, song and dancing? Everyone must join in, my lively Angie also, and even Mumsy as chaperone.

That year Mr. Camilo Padilla, president of the Centro de Cultura, still full of energy and civic interest in spite of his crippled condition, brought the Spanish Señorita, Velasquez, to teach the fancy Spanish dances. At fiesta time she gave a dance program with her well-trained pupils. Angie, wearing my yellow silk gauze gown, and her partner, Pablito, in his black velvet Charro costume, danced the fancy *Samaqueca* so gracefully that they won first prize. "The boys are calling me the queen," Angie told me. "Well, don't be such a proud señorita," I advised her.

CHAPTER XXIII

Angelina at Boarding School

The fourth of September found me at the bus station, parting with my daughter for the first time. She was leaving me to enter the academy school in Albuquerque. Both of us were almost in tears as she kissed me good-bye, saying: "Hurry up and come." I had promised to rent my house and go and rent an apartment in Albuquerque and have her stay with me.

Her letters came often, full of news. She had been out with a girl friend she had met there and had looked at some apartments. "Come before these are rented," she wrote. But she came home for the Christmas vacation and found me still here. The person who had rented my house was leaving soon, and this changed my plan about going down.

However, Angie had the happiest school term as a boarder. Like her father, she made friends everywhere she went. She became very fond of her dancing teacher, Miss Kahnt, and wrote about the pleasant visits she had on weekends at Miss Kahnt's home. The teacher had also become very much interested in Angie and invited her to go with her that summer on her vacation to visit her sister, who was a professional dancer in Hollywood. I was opposed to Angie's becoming a dancer and changed their plans, suggesting that instead they invite two or more of their friends and go and spend a few weeks at our country home. Each one must take

143

her own dishes and bedding. I went ahead to put in some furniture.

The girls arrived in a hurry, before I had finished. Eleanor Marron had a sort of disappointed look when she saw the big empty house. The look had worn off by the end of two weeks when, thinking their groceries must be giving out, I went to take the girls home. They were so happy. The neighbors had been grand to them, entertaining them at their homes and with picnics and moonlight hayrides. Reluctantly they left, with hopes of again returning the following summer. Each summer, as soon as school had closed, Angie looked forward to these happy vacations out in the country. Mrs. Martin knowing this, when she came for her daughter one year, took Angie. It was the first time Angie had been away from me. After four days I could not stand being without her. I wrote her to come home that Saturday. She was so obedient that she came. "Mrs. Martin was really angry at you," she said. "She had planned to give us a picnic at Chama this Sunday." I realized how it must have hurt Angie to miss it, and it hurt me, too.

All our friends were so kind to her. The Clarks in Santa Fe had taken her on picnics at Las Vegas and Taos and other places. The Bacas had taken her to their country home at Rociada. One summer I left her with her aunt at El Rito while I went to Santa Fe to attend to some business. Her cousins, the Sargents, came along and invited her to accompany them to the wedding of a cousin of theirs at Monte Vista, Colorado. The bride was the daughter of my friend, Odila, whose wedding I had attended at San Luis before my marriage.

Angie came back, gleefully telling me: "Everybody was so nice! Your *comadre,* Odila, would catch me and draw me onto her lap and ask me all about you. Emilio, her son, came along, and taking me by the arm, said, 'Come, Angie, let's go and have some cake.' I did not know how to act. Here, at home, everyone is so cold."

We are a reserved family. Our love is a restrained, formal one. She was the emotional, affectionate kind, like her father, and must have longed for that warm, demonstrative love, which she did not receive from her family.

How disappointed Angie was and how much I regretted when we found I could not afford to again send her to the Albuquerque school where she had been so happy. For some unexplainable reason, I did not like to see Angie on the streets so much that year, going and coming from school. She understood, however, that boarding schools are expensive and that with the estate yet unsettled, we had to live carefully. Another reason was that it did not seem to me quite fair, since the Loretto Sisters of Santa Fe had been so kindly considerate while teaching her all the previous years, that she should now go to be graduated at another school.

With her usual resignation, she went back to Loretto, trying to be contented, but not happy.

One of the boarders said, "Angie is so different this year." "In what way?" I asked her. "I don't know, but she is," the girl answered.

Yes, my dear girl misses her dear teacher, Sister Florian, and her friend Margaret. Margaret was such a sweet girl, full of pure, innocent wit.

My friend, Marguerite Baca, was having a tea, and invited Angie to help serve. Here again her pink chiffon gown seemed so becoming to her that a lady doctor from out of town to whom we were introduced, asked me, "Have you ever had your daughter's picture painted? You ought to have it now, while she has this lovely, fresh complexion." I saw Mrs. Otero leading Angie by the hand through the crowd of guests to introduce her to ex-Governor Otero. Angie was looking so pleased that it made my heart swell.

As we came back to the house from the party, Angie said, "Well, I have attended my first real party." "Yes," I replied, "and you were quite successful, it seemed. I don't want to make you feel any prouder, but I am going to tell you of a compliment which Dr. D. paid you. She told me I ought to have your picture painted while you yet have this lovely, fresh complexion. "You see, if you were going out at night, smoking, drinking and dancing, you would not look as nice and fresh. Some of the girls there who are just in their teens look old already."

With my old-fashioned strict ideas still inbedded in me I had tried to bring up my daughter in the old Spanish rule, sheltered in her home. One evening my nephew invited her to the movie. I said, 'No, Fernando, I don't allow Angie to go out at night. You may take her to the matinee some afternoon." It was not for want of confidence; Fernando was the best boy I have ever known. "You are so hard on poor Angelina," Mother told me. Feeling a sense of guilt, I confess I was too severe and even cold. I only showed the duty and care and not the love which was the real motive prompting my actions. Angie was eighteen years old and still did not know what a night party or dance was except those they had at the convent. Her friends who were already popular with boy friends would ask me, "When are you going to let Angie go out with her friends?" I said: "There is plenty of time for that when she finishes school." "Mother will have to become gay again and learn to dance, for I know she will want to chaperone me," Angie added. Although she seemed to take it in this pleasant way, I now feel that to have been kept so restricted must have kept her in an inner conflict with herself, trying to please me and longing for the freedom she saw her friends have. My mistake was, I see, that in trying to keep her free from gossip and innocent of wordly knowledge, I had failed to see that she was living in a different age, when girls were not so submissive as in my time. Perhaps I was too much against the modern codes, and fashion fads. "I am the only one who wears long stockings, and no one in this town suits you," she said when I forbade her going with girls who were not the kind I ever had associated with. She always had an answer ready, where I had quietly listened to my mother and thought her always right. Her faults were "passe," but I was demanding perfection. With stubborn determination I was trying to mold her life to my liking, ignoring the important dogma of psychology that each individual has a right to be himself as nature has endowed him. "You never see what I do right," she told me once. Yes, I did see, but I thought it a duty to do the right thing. I despise flattery, but a little praise and more patience on my part would have helped her check those temperamental outbursts. She was so sensitive about being corrected and cried so easily, it irritated me. My nerves were already overwrought with so many sorrows and cares. It was trying, to have her come late from school when I had errands for her to attend. She had so many excuses — choir, plays, music — all required practice. "Bring your bed, Angeline," Mother Bernard would tell her when she saw her there long after school hours.

CHAPTER XXIV

La Placita Tea Room

Soon Angie found a new interest by helping my sister in a Spanish tea room she had opened at *La Placita*. Angie enjoyed meeting the nice people and was so thrilled at the compliments she received in her becoming *China poblana* costume, which I made for her to wear. Nevertheless, I felt that she was doing too much. On this, her senior year, her studies were heavy, and to have to rush home, set tables, help prepare some of the food and serve tables for three hours was hard work. I helped her wash flower bowls and arrange fresh flowers in them, refilled sugar bowls and salt shakers, served plates and put away food. Yet I heard complaints about her not helping enough. I would not hurt her feelings by telling her. It has always been that way — my family taking for granted all I have ever done for them. The little that others do is always greatly appreciated.

Angie, however, was happy to be earning her own pin money. Her first investment was the purchase of a copy of "Caballeros," by my friend, Ruth L. Barker. With this gift, she pleased me on my birthday, the first of November. Next, she treated herself to a pair of riding trousers for which she had been wishing. I had not bought them for her because we were divided in our opinions as to the style, I wanting the full-cuff style and she the tight-fitting leg. She won, and I had to admit to myself that she really looked cute in them,

148

wearing them with her white blouse, black silk necktie and Ven's ranch hat. I was sorry I had given away her father's derby and high black silk hat before she grew up.

Not forgetting her dear dancing teacher, Angie wrote to Miss Kahnt, inviting her to come as her dinner guest to *La Placita,* and spend the night with us. Angie was looking for an opportunity to ask her to start a dancing class here at Loretto, and was delighted when, in the morning, she took Miss Kahnt to introduce her to Sister Bernard. Arrangements and permission from Sister were obtained for her to teach one class a week. This gave Angie an opportunity to continue her dancing lessons and to have her dear teacher visit with her once a week.

One morning my neighbor, Mrs. Clark, came in to tell me I should cover the windows. "Cover your windows," she said. "We can see Angie dancing in here from our house, and this morning I found a man's footprints under Mia's window. I traced them over to your alley, but lost them there." I said: "On these deep, high windows I cannot reach to pull down the shades, and who would come to bother us? I have never even seen that peeping Tom, whom people have seen around the neighborhood, looking in their windows." Later, I told her that I wished I had followed her advice, for not long after someone was seen at my window; but I did not hear about it until too late.

There is a superstition among the Spanish people that when a white flower blooms in the house, someone in the family is going to die. Not believing superstitions, I kept for years a box of white geraniums blooming. My Aunt Lucia had given me the slips. The plants had belonged to her daughter, who had passed away. My Aunt said it made her feel sad to see them.

One fall I left the geranium box on the porch, and the plants froze. The stems wilted and dropped. As I was coming into the house about the last week in October, I noticed a little white flower on the end of a wilted stem. "Look,

Angie," I said, "at that geranium, still trying to bloom. I have treated it so badly and have left it out here to freeze; yet it refuses to die and, like my twice-frozen fern, springs to life again from the roots.

Before long, fate dealt me another sad blow to dampen my spirits. My poor gentle mother, who, like my husband, had for so many years suffered her ills with such sweet patience, now ceased to suffer.

To show in what great esteem she had been held by all her household of servants, one evening some months after she had passed away, my little nephew came running in to tell me that there was a man sitting on our front porch steps, crying. I called to my brother, Alfonso, to come down to see what could be the matter with the poor man. I was surprised to see Alfonso coming in, holding Erineo by the arm. He was still crying. He had just been discharged from a hospital in Colorado, and at Arroyo Hondo he learned of my mother's death, and had come to see us. Feeling the emptiness he would now find in the home, he broke down and sat and cried outside. My brothers loved him and called him *"manito neito."*

On October 6, my sister loaned Angie the tea room in which to hold her birthday party. I suggested that she borrow a phonograph and ask the girls she was inviting to bring their boy friends, so they could dance. I said, "By noon when you come, I shall have the other things ready, and you may help me mix the cake."

"Yes, I will ask Sister to let me out earlier from school," she said, quite pleased. But at noon when she came, she had changed her mind. Eating her lunch, she had to leave in a hurry to buy the favors she wished to give the girls.

"I have the oven heated and we mix the cake now, or you will have to make your own cake," I said.

When she came after school and saw no cake — I was busy fixing the fruit punch and other things — she picked up the cake ingredients and went to my mother's and asked my sister, in a crying fit, to help her make the cake. She had

150

never done any cooking herself, except to fix eggs and toast.

I had the table fixed very pretty with flowers and candles, but Angie's red eyes and sad look hurt me. She was not her happy self, which she had always been at her parties.

A few weeks after school had opened, a relative from the country stopped to see me. He was very much worried because the nuns had refused to take his daughter, who had been partly paying for her school expenses by helping the sisters after school. "Leave Marie here with me; she may attend as a day scholar," I told him. I felt sorry for him, as he had lost so much during the depression.

I took Angie's bed and left my double bed so that the girls might sleep together in my room. As the weather became colder, Angie complained, "Marie pulls all the blankets away from me, and I wake up uncovered and so cold. Let me sleep in the front room. I love that bright room," she begged. Later, I remembered what mother said to me after Angie, feeling so thrilled, had told her about my fixing up the front bedroom for her. "And are you going to let Angelina sleep alone in that room?" my mother asked. "Oh, no, but she needs a room in which to keep her nice things and for her girl friends when they come to visit her." Angie kept on pleading until I said, a little impatiently, "All right, and as soon as the weather gets warm, I am going to fix up the back porch into a sleeping porch for you, so we shall be close together." She was thrilled, saying, "I am going to start making scarves and drapes in rose and with my ivory bedroom set brought over from Grandma's, I shall fix it lovely."

Every night before going to bed, I would go into the living room by her room and turn the key sideways, so it could not be pushed out of the lock from the outside and another key inserted to open the door. I had told her "Angie, pull your shades all the way down, so anyone who may be passing cannot look in, as you are now right on the street."

After my mother's death, I asked Angie not to play any music for awhile. The Spanish people are very strict about

151

observing mourning; some might hear it and think we had no feeling.

Friday, on her way home from school, Angie came through my father's house on her daily visit to the family. As she stood at the door of my sister's room, she said, "I feel so queer!" "Like what?" my sister asked. "I don't know," Angie answered, looking very pale and sad as she turned and left the room. That day I had a woman washing the windows and when Angie came in, I told her I was so tired that I had not finished locking the windows and screens. "I will lock them," she said. The next day as I was coming from the grocery, I saw the dressing room window screen lying on the ground. "Pick up that screen, Marie," I said, "and take it to the back porch. I have been wanting to have it fixed, as it has a crack through which a knife can be slipped to unlock it." The following day being Sunday, the screen was forgotten and the locking of the window also. That window was filled with a big potted cactus plant and my heavy typewriter and, who would have thought anyone would be so daring as to break through a window on the front side of the house?

Sunday morning, upon our return from church, Angie asked me, sitting at the piano, "May I play, mother?" The touch of sadness and the low voice in which she asked me, so different from her usual cheerful self, touched me. I answered, trying to seem cheerful, "Yes, do; you will be forgetting your music." She opened the piano, ran her fingers listelessly over the keyboard, closed the piano and left the room. How strange she was acting. She always went through several pieces and song before she stopped.

After luncheon, the three of us sat around the dining table, reading. Then I said, "It's such a nice day, Marie; you come with me to Doña Leandra's. I want to show you where she lives so you will know where to go when I want to send you there. And you, Angie, put away your book and go out in the fresh air. You are losing your eyesight from reading so much."

152

LA PLACITA TEA ROOM

"Yes, I am going to see the girls at the convent," she said, putting away her book.

Marie and I found poor blind Leandra and her blind sister locked in, as usual. We had to tell her who we were before she would open the door. "And, where is my *comadrita*, Angelina?" she asked, greeting us. "When she comes, she always asks me to tell her a story, and I make her sing me a song first, while I think of some funny *chiste* to tell her, as I know no stories," Leandra told us.

On our way back from Leandra's, we stopped at my father's house. "Angie came through here and asked me to tell you that she is waiting for you at Mrs. Clark's," my sister told me. Just then the phone rang. It was Angie, saying, "Mumsy, the Clarks have invited me to go to Lamy with them." I replied, "Oh, Angie, I have come back so tired that I want you to see about supper." "You rest and I shall be back to fix it. Mrs. Clark says it will take only half an hour to get there," came her reply.

Six o'clock, seven, and no Angie. Marie helped me prepare supper and we had just seated ourselves at the table when Angie "blew in" out of breath — just like a "cyclone," I used to tell her. "Late as usual." "Let me tell you, Mumsy," she started. "Get your plate and come and tell us all about it," I interrupted. She continued, "Well, while we were at Lamy, the Santa Fe Pullman train came in, and Mr. Clark, being an engineer, took Mia and me and showed us through the engine and the cars. What a little toy our D. & R. G. engine is compared to the huge engine on that train." "Yes," I said, "and to think that Ven and I were always traveling on those fine trains, and now I only go to El Rito." "Never mind, Mumsy, as soon as I finish school, I am going to work, save money for one year and, then, we shall travel; work again and travel." "Yes, I want you to see some of the nice places I have seen," I told her.

After supper we again sat around the dining table, the girls preparing their lessons and I reading until bedtime; then we picked up our books and each went to her own room. Angie came back tying the belt on her robe. She

153

leaned against the radiator in front of the bathroom door. I was washing my hands, and looked up at her, noting that she was wearing the new silk pajamas which her aunt had just sent her from Denver. I said, "There you are, wearing your best, which you should be saving for visiting." She looked down at them and, with a queer, little smile, turned and went back to her room without a word — not even her customary goodnight. I was surprised, but thought I had vexed her, and went to bed.

CHAPTER XXV

A Night of Horror

Destiny, still not satisfied, seemed bent on crushing me down to the very last of my endurance. Now it dealt me the hardest blow a mother may suffer. Three weeks after parting with my dear mother, a most heartbreaking tragedy, one that horrified every citizen not only in this city of Santa Fe, but throughout the state, fell upon me like a piercing dagger, cutting through the very core of my heart and soul.

After seventeen years of praying for strength and resignation, I am now finding the courage to tell about this most terrible tragedy — not for the curious, but to let the truth be known and dispel suspicion on some other person. There were some false stories told by ignorant people, always ready to invent lies. Those who knew my daughter and my family knew better than to believe them. When I read the story someone told me was published in a detective magazine, I was so shocked. Who had dared to give them such information? I was the only one who knew the truth of what had happened. My family tried to keep me from hearing about the newspapers and all the publicity, but others were not so considerate. Years after, people were still telling me, "I have the magazine with your daughter's picture," or "I have a daughter named for her." Yes, the name I thought I had invented to please Sister Angelica was now a favorite one. They told me it means virgin and martyr; but my heart

155

would sink everytime someone came up to me in a public place and mentioned her name.

I have said before how Angie had skipped locking the screen and window in the dressing room. Like myself, I suppose she thought no one could come through it, as it was so well blocked. But it was through this least suspected window, so full of obstacles, that the one who had been seen lurking around windows in the vicinity, since he had been freed from the penitentiary, crawled in and smothered the life out of my beloved daughter.

What can still the hand of fate? Not even prayer for protection, as we had prayed for this, night and morning. It is something one cannot understand nor escape, but must endure.

I had been so careful every night when I awakened about 11:30 to look in Angie's room. This Sunday night, tired from my walks to church and to blind Leandra's home, I slept soundly until a flash of bright light on my eyes awakened me. "Angie!" I called, opening my eyes but seeing nothing but darkness. That seemed so strange. Had not someone just now lit the light in the kitchen? I lit the candle on the little table by my bed, slipped on my slippers, took the candle and stepped into the kitchen, finding the dining room door still swinging. Someone had just gone through it. Slowly I pushed the door open. Seeing no one, I placed the candle on the table and, then, noticed the light in Angie's room. Cautiously I walked through the living room, held back the portiere, which someone had drawn over the opening between that room and her bedroom. A horrified scream escaped me as I saw before me, standing by Angie's bed the broad shoulders of a man in black and white shirt (not the coveralls they showed at the court trial). Startled by my scream, his shoulders gave a quick shrug. I imagine he sprang at me and caught me by the throat, for my throat later felt sore all night. Fortunately, as I screamed, my eyes closed in a faint and I was spared the terrible fright of seeing his face, which like those black and white stripes, would have been impressed upon my mind, making me shudder every time I see a dark face.

The next thing I saw, as my eyes opened for just a second, was the corner of the dining room wall. My eyes must have been dilated with fright: the wall looked glaringy white. I screamed in a horrible voice "Marie!" and knew nothing more. I had fallen in a faint by the dining room table. The man must have released his grasp on my throat, to run after Marie, as he caught sight of her running out the kitchen door to tell Mrs. Clark, my neighbor.

How long I lay there I don't know. As I began coming to, I felt something rough on my cheek, and felt around with my hand, wondering why I was lying on the rug at my bed-side. Then, like a flash, there came to me the thought of what I had seen in my daughter's room, and I sprang up and ran to her room. From the opening I turned back, horrified at the ghastly sight which met my glance. There was my daughter stretched across the bed, her face covered with a pillow. Mute with fright, I ran back to my room. At the door I discovered that Marie's bed was empty. Grabbing the little blanket at the foot of my bed to wrap around me, I stepped back into the kitchen and saw that the back door was ajar. "They took her out through here," I thought. I closed the door with a feeling of terrible horror, afraid someone would push it back in my face. Through the other door of the kitchen, I ran out on the front porch, at the end of which I met two men turning in. I stopped, calling, "Hurry! My daughter!"

"What! Have they taken her?" one of the men asked as we went into the kitchen.

"No, she is in there," I said, pointing to the dining room door.

One of the men went in and the other took me by the arm into my room and sat by me, holding me on my bed. I was crying so much that I did not notice when the man left. My brother and sister were now sitting on each side of me, holding me. "Call a doctor," someone said in the kitchen.

"What doctor shall I call, Doctor Ward Livingston?"

Mrs. Clark asked me. I saw her standing against the door
frame, Marie, still in her night gown and with bare feet,
standing by her, looking extremely pale.

"Livingston or anyone," I answered. "Why didn't you
come sooner? I asked her. She only hung her head and left.

Very soon, Dr. Livingston was standing in front of me,
asking for a towel. I looked in the mirror of my dressing
table, and shook with fright at the sight of my bloody face
and gown. I had not even felt that I was hurt until the doctor started to bandage the cut on my head.

"Wrap her up and take her to the hospital. My car is out
in front," he said to my brother. Some strong arms carried
me out to the car and into the hospital, laying me on the
bed. All through the rest of the night I had nausea and
choking spells, feeling as if I could not get my breath or
swallow even water.

The sad day dawned. My sincere old friend, Margaret,
came in and relieved my sister from her watch at my bed-
side. Later, my three brothers from Taos came in. My good
neighbors, the Martins, from El Rito, were there earlier. No
one seemed to know what to say, and I could only cry. Marguerite stayed with me all night and all the next day. In the
evening of the second day, when my brothers came in to see
me again, Marguerite said, "Mr. Sayer says he will come in
the morning and take you to see Angelina, if you wish." I
hestiated.

"Yes, you had better see her. She looks so beautiful. I
have already prayed to her," my brother Tom said to me.

I replied, "I shall let you know in the morning. Stay
with me tonight, Tom, and *Comadre Margarita,* you go and
take a rest."

The next morning Marguerite was back. I told her,
"You may tell Mr. Sayer to come for me." I had prayed for
strength all night. Lying on a cot, I was wheeled into the
living room at my father's home. The room was like a floral
shop, filled with perfume from the floral tributes banked all
around the room.

"You have many friends, Mrs. Jaramillo," Mr. Sayer said

A NIGHT OF HORROR

as he led me to the casket. For a moment I looked down at my dear Angie. Yes, she looked sweet and so natural, as if in a happy dream. She was dressed in the pale pink chiffon dress, all of which I had made by hand for her for the junior-senior banquet. As I looked down at her pale hands, I realized that she was not just asleep, but that she was now leaving me, and that this was my last look at my dear one. I felt faint. Mr. Sayer and Marguerite led me to my cot and then took me back to the hospital.

After five days I was longing to be with my family. The doctor said I could be taken home. My brother, Ben, and my sister came for me, taking me and placing me in a bed by my father's bed. For more than a week I lay there, too weak and disheartened to care to live. I tried to pray, but my heart was too grieved. All I could do was to ask our god to forgive me and to accept my tears as a prayer. Shock and desolation had come upon me. I was about to give up when I received a letter from a dear friend, saying, "Dear friend, no matter what this cruel world does to us, it cannot take the love of God from us." Yes, I still had the love of God, and this counted more than everything else. He did not send me this trial. He only permitted it, perhaps, to open my eyes that I might become better, more humble and forgiving.

So many kind letters, prayers and verses composed by friends were sent to me, that they made me think the world was full of good people. My heart grew more resigned. Had this great grief not come into my life I would never have known that great reservoir of kindness, which has grown into the wide friendship I meet on every side, not only in my home town but in every place I visit.

(Composed by Mrs. Dolores Otero Berg)

"She is not dead but sleepeth" —
Sweetly and tenderly at rest,
With the understanding arms beneath her,
Her white soul beloved and blessed.

159

"She is not dead but sleepeth;"
In the garden of God she lives,
And the scent of her flower-like spirit,
Still upholds the heart that grieves.

"She is not dead but sleepeth;"
And why should you mourn and weep?
She lives eternally in God,
So sleep, Angeline, sleep!

(Composed by Mrs. George Martin)

She was ushered into the world
Like a great princess of old;
There's an heiress, there's an heiress,
Kind friends were told.

She was guarded by a mother
Who was gentle kind and true,
Who could think of nothing better
With her time that she could do.

Her father was a colonel
Of that proud Spanish type,
And was taken from his dear ones
When his heyday time was ripe.

Why this cruel, sad departure?
God alone can understand;
There was no one less deserving,
If we'd search throughout the land.

To this gentle, kind, true mother,
All our sympathy goes to,
And our little martyr, Angelina,
A loving, long adieu.

And now came the awful court trial of the accused. I was summoned to appear as a witness and my cousin, Blanche, came and took my sister and me to the courthouse. District Attorney Kenney led me by the arm to the witness chair. I

160

could only testify that I had not seen the man's face. A man's life was at stake; I could not lie. Some people thought I could have said that I had seen his face. Marie also said she had only seen the figure of a man, as his arm brushed the candle off the dining table. It extinguished as it fell on the rug, or it would have set me on fire.

Our testimonies of not having seen his face encouraged the criminal to deny his guilt and to carry on his fight for freedom, but there was strong evidence against him. On the base of my beautiful gold inlaid Venetian vase that he grabbed from the piano to hit me on the head, he had left his fingerprints. After the policemen and detective gathered the evidence they could find at my house, they went to the nearest garage to get gas in their car. There they found the night watchman lying on the floor half unconcious from blows he had received on his head by a man who had come in and stolen a car. The injured man was sent to the hospital, and the police followed the tracks of the thief who had stolen the car. They found him having an early breakfast in a restaurant in Albuquerque. They brought him back by a different road and placed him in safekeeping at the penitentiary.

Men friends of my father's came and offered to do whatever he said, but my father was a peaceful man and told them to let the law take care of the case.

During the trial, the attorney for the defense tried to introduce the point that I could not have seen the light in my daughter's room five rooms away. That was the light which hit my eyes like a flash of lightning, awakening me that awful, eventful night. I thought it had come from the kitchen, but when I opened my eyes everything was dark. This puzzled me.

It was some years after when the mystery was cleared up. One night when the light had been lit in the dining room and the door to the kitchen was open, I went into my bedroom. As I bent to get something out of the dresser drawer, the brightest ray of light hit my eyes. Looking up, I saw a bright reflection from the glass on a picture of little Virginia that hung over the radiator by the corner wall where I had fallen on the rug. The glass was catching the light from the open door into the kitchen, and reflecting it to the mirror of the dresser, where it was reflected again in a slant to my face! This had to be seen to be believed. Both attorneys had passed away before the puzzle solved itself. The intruder had come into the dining room, lit the light before closing the door, turned the light out immediately and gone back to stand by the bed where I had seen his back. How strangely things had worked out.

Promptly, the New York Life Insurance Company agent came to pay me Angie's policy. I left the money with the company. I could not force myself to touch what I had sacrificed to save for my daughter. In October I had told her there were only two more premiums to pay. "When the policy matures, I am going to leave the money in escrow so you will get an allowance of just so much a month."

"Fine idea — so I won't blow it all in at once," she said.

A few months after the culprit was sent to the electric chair, his attorney, who had conscientiously defended him, sent a communication to the editor of our leading newspaper. It read in part as follows:

Santa Fe, N. M.
Jan. 26, 1931

Mr. Editor:

I am not at all satisfied with the aftermath of the Johnson case, referring to the little publicity given to a most striking instance of public self control — one, I am inclined to think, of the most remarkable in the history of crime and its persecution in this country.

The crime was most fiendish and horrifying — none could be more so, committed in the center of the capital city of the state, in the early part of the night, in proximity to houses of several neighbors still awake. This devilish bold-

A NIGHT OF HORROR

ness of the criminal added force to the public shock, and yet the people of the city, under a nervous tension that generally super-induces an irresistible impulse to immediately convene the court of Judge Lynch, contained themselves, kept their heads, permitted the alleged criminal to remain safely under custody, accorded him every right under the law, both by the court and the district attorney. The counsel for the defense was courteously given every opportunity to present his case. Under the circumstances the people of Santa Fe and the surrounding country are justly entitled to have their self-control and observance of law published to the world in blazing headlines, and to be congratulated on their steadiness under circumstances more grievous than any that have occurred, or likely to occur again, in the history of New Mexico.

As a citizen, I for one am patting myself on the back because I live in a town of such level-headed, law-abiding people. We of this capital city are abundantly entitled to paraphrase Little Jack Horner as we pull a plum out of the pie and say, "Oh, what great people we are."

I am proudly yours,

H. Crist.

On Thanksgiving Day, my cousin, Blanche, came to take me to have dinner with her. "Wrap up and come; only Gonzalo will be there," she told me. She could not have chosen a brighter day to bring me out of my dark confinement. For a month I had seen only sad faces come to my bedside to offer sympathy.

We rode along Hillside Avenue. Just the night before winter set in, leaving the world clad in a blanket of glittering snow from the high *Sangre de Cristo* Mountains to the evergreen-covered hills and the city's streets. New Mexico sunshine from a spotless blue heaven blinded us with its brilliancy. It was a scene to which not even an anguished heart like mine could shut its sense of feeling.

My cousin's home reflected her simple good taste. It was bright and cheerful, and her sweet boy, who had cried, "No,

163

I don't want to see her with her head cut up," was now happy to see me. I had a nice, silk scarf draped over my head, and I tried to be cheerful and enjoy my cousin's good cooking. Tears must be shed in the heart, in secret, and like St. Monica, we must meet the world with a smile.

From that day forward a change began coming over me. I again felt my love for that pure beauty which fills the world and like a tonic injected into me, it lifted my spirits. For the day I forgot my bitter cup.

Some weeks after, when I took courage to go out for a walk, the sun seemed to have lost its bright rays and the whole world to be in an eclipse. I could not lift my head until some kind person passing me would speak to me.

My little four-old niece, Virginia, was the only cheering tonic at home. Every night before going to bed, she would come to my door and ask, "Shall I dance for you?" Looking like a beautiful angel in her flowing white nightie, her dimpled arms outspread like wings, her long golden curls like a golden halo framing her beautiful face, she would flit gracefully all around the room, singing and dancing until she bowed herself out at the door and disappeared like a beautiful apparition, leaving my mind in a state of relaxation.

Gradually I started going back to my home, although the first time I went into Angie's room and saw her things everywhere, the pain was almost unbearable. Horror crept through me every time I passed the dressing room door, or saw the window, even from across the street. "Take that room out," my sister advised." "No, I need it," I answered. I had faced things which were much harder to face than the presence of this room. I could bear this.

The hardest task now was to part with my daughter's things. The piano, the Edison phonograph and her ukelele went first, for music brings more tears when the heart is sorrowing, especially when associated with the dear ones who have departed from us.

Fifteen years have passed and I still hold on to some of the books and things she loved most. Gathering our personal possessions to pack them away, clearing the closets and drawers, so as to rent the house, for I could not stay in it for more than a few hours at a time, I found Angie's bulging memory book, full of clever writings, pictures, letters. There was one letter addressed to herself as "Sister?? — Mrs. ?? — or Miss 26??" The letter was sealed. It is a long letter and reads partly:

> Are you still Miss, nun, or Mrs.? I hope still Miss at home with Mumsy. Lonesome? I never dream. Has Mother kept you as she used to? You are supporting her nicely, I hope. Don't forget your dear school chum, friend Margaret Ortiz. Keep praying to her to help you. You need it. Please be true to dear Loretto and your Alma Mater. Best of all for you.

> Gobs of love to my undiscovered (as yet) self.

> Miss 16

*   *   *   *   *   *

Among the clippings cut out of newspapers and glued in her book was one which reads partly " 'El Jaramillo' is the name plastered on the side of one of the Santa Fe's newest all-steel Pullman observation cars, which passed through Albuquerque on the California Limited for the first time today. 'El Jaramillo' is a beauty, finished in the most exquisite of polished woods and with about every device for safety and comfort. It is the first of a series of cars which will be named for famous families in the Southwest. This particular car has the name of former Colonel Venceslao Jaramillo, the successor of one of the most noted Spanish families in the Southwest, etc."

This and other newspaper articles written and published about her father fired in her, family pride. She had kept them.

Consoling herself about her small stature, she had

165

another article: "Small stature is no detriment to great achievements," mentioning Napoleon and other great men not much over four feet high.

CHAPTER XXVI

Only by Trying Do We Learn

And here in a drawer I find the manuscript of the book which my daughter had encouraged me to start writing. Hearing of the customs of my girlhood days, she would say, "How interesting! I never heard of this before. Why don't you write it?" This gave me food for thought. True, this new generation knew nothing of our interesting old customs. These would soon be lost if someone did not put them down in writing.

My sister also kept saying, "Someone ought to write these beautiful children's stories which Mother tells." Yes, someone who can write. I never could. When strict Sister Dolorine would say, "Don't you girls come to me with a one-page composition!" it scared me, because no matter how hard I racked my brain, I could never write more. However, writing and art are contagious in this old town. We have caught the fever from our famous *"cinco pintores"* and author Mary Austin, and some of us have the courage to try. It is only by trying that we learn what we can do.

Although I had not heard mother's stories since before I started attending boarding school, I yet remembered more than twenty-five of her stories. After translating the first story, I discovered that it was not so difficult, and soon I had twenty-six stories translated into English and published in book form under the title, *Spanish Fairy Tales*. I had to

167

omit some of the repetitions which I used to think made the stories more interesting. The change of voice and the expression of the storyteller added much, also.

My next attempt was in writing a cook book, called *New Mexico Tasty Recipes*. I now felt so encouraged that I completed the writing of my book on folklore, *Shadows of the Past*. This was a difficult task. I had the material, but like a builder without experience, did not know how to put it together. I tried sending my manuscript to some of our Western universities. After holding it for several months, they would return it, saying they did not have the funds with which to publish it. One professor said he was writing a book. Would I permit him to use two or three of my stories in his book? I then understood. All they wanted was to read my manuscript and get ideas from it, so I decided to have it published by a small private press here in my city.

Its sale has increased each year, and I feel that I have accomplished at least one thing — preserved in writing our rapidly vanishing New Mexico Spanish folk customs. Persons who have read my book and are doing research work come to me for help from all over our states. This shows that our folk customs are found to be interesting. Two nuns who were sent out here from the Philadelphia University to write a Spanish play, called me to say they were coming to see me. One was big and tall, and the first thing she said when she saw me at the door, "Isn't she little?" If she were disappointed in my looks, she was quite interested in my books and kept hinting that she would like to get copies of them, until I gave her a copy of each book. I asked Mr. Dendahl if he would show these nuns, as well as those at Loretto, the fine movie pictures of the Santa Fe Fiesta which he had shown the members of the *Sociedad Folklorica* at one of our meetings. He was nice enough to do this at Loretto Convent. The sisters were so fascinated by the colorful fiesta pictures, they remained here about a month longer in order that they might see the fiesta. Some months afterwards, the nun who was writing the play wrote, asking me for more information in regard to the work of my folklore society and

ONLY BY TRYING DO WE LEARN

also for a brief history of my life and work. She wished to write these in her book. I have never heard any more about her work.

CHAPTER XXVII

The Santa Fe Fiesta

It's now the year 1935 in the present city of Santa Fe, but the calendar has been turned back to the year 1672 to commemorate the re-conquest of the capital of the Royal Kingdom of New Spain. There is a great contrast between the weary remnants of the army of Gen. Diego de Vargas which entered the city in that year and the resplendent De Vargas pageant now entering the city, as also is the gay, colorful crowd which fills the capital today to celebrate its annual fiesta, commemorating his victory. Many additions have lately been brought about to make it a genuine Spanish fiesta. It now starts with the burning of *Zozobra*, the Spanish effigy of gloom. Into the huge image are placed all the afflictions and troubles of mankind. Amid loud grunts and groans and the hissing and spitting of fire, Zozobra burns, writhing in agony. The crowd, being freed of all its troubles, flocks back to the plaza to witness the formal crowning of the queen of the fiesta, as she sits attired in rich velvet on her royal throne, surrounded by her court.

The celebrant representing Gen. de Vargas arises and places the jeweled crown on the fair brow of the Spanish señorita who has been elected to be the fiesta queen. Everyone now enters into the spirit of the fiesta. The socialites fill the cocktail and the lounge rooms at the La Fonda Hotel. Town and country people, laughing and chatting, shove

THE SANTA FE FIESTA

their way around the plaza and into colorful booths to satisfy their appetites with the piquant Spanish dishes served *al fresco*. Music and song and the sound of dancing fills the air. Even the eyes of the elders sparkle with the merrymaking. Reluctantly, the crowds retire to resume the next day with Sunday's traditional religious celebration. The Spaniards always left a blend of religion with their history. History tells us that, before attacking the Indians, Gen. de Vargas made a vow that if the Indians were defeated and the conquest won, he would build a chapel in honor of Our Lady *"Conquistadora"* whose image he carried with his army. Twelve years later Capt. Gen. Marquez de la Peñuela ordained that the city council contribute a sum of money to pay for vespers and mass to be celebrated as a thanksgiving for the victory won. The order is still complied with. In a long, colorful procession the archbishop is escorted from his residence to the cathedral, where he celebrates a solemn, high mass, sung by forty seminarian voices. The impressive sermon is preached by some eloquent visiting prelate.

On Sunday afternoon we again see the brave De Vargas and his knights in their rich velvet and silk costumes, plumed hats and shining shields, helmeted soldiers and the gray hooded monks entering the capital, followed by the conquered Indians. The monks again plant the cross of Christianity in front of the old Palace of the Governors. After evening vespers, burning *luminarias* light the way for hundreds of people in the candlelight procession wending its way to the cross of the martyrs erected on the summit of the Hill of *Cuma*. It is a beautiful sight, with the flickering candle lights, like a firefly necklace winding itself around the hill, and the light of the *luminarias* silhouetting the cross against the dark, starlit sky. A sermon is preached by the archbishop, bringing to memory the lives of the heroic twenty-one Franciscan missionaries who lost their lives in the Indian rebellion while bringing the light of Christian faith to these heathens.

On Monday morning the children's pet parade takes

171

place and, in the afternoon the historical parade amuses the populace. A fitting end to this gay, three-day celebration is the *Conquistadores'* Ball, attended by a large crowd of formally-attired socialites. Aside from the historical nature of the celebration, many social events precede the fiesta.

CHAPTER XXVIII

Spanish Folklore Society Organized

Several years had passed since parting with my dear family, and time and faith, healers of all wounds, were lifting the shadows which enshrouded me and which otherwise would have been too heavy for me to bear.

While calling upon and taking one of my Spanish recipe cookbooks to one of my neighbors, our conversation for the moment centered around Spanish recipes. "Have you seen the article in *Holland Magazine* written by Mrs. D?" she inquired. I had not seen it, so she gave me the magazine to take home to read it. It was a three-page article, nicely written and illustrated, but very deficient as to knowledge of our Spanish cooking. In giving the recipe for making *tortillas* it read, "Mix bread flour with water, add salt." How nice and light these must be without yeast or shortening! And still these smart Americans make money with their writing, and we who know the correct way sit back and listen.

Here was another interesting article about the Natchez pilgrimage celebrated annually in that city. The city's history sounds similar to our city's history in that, like Santa Fe, it had had three different changes of government — British, Spanish and now American. The fusing of the three national ideals left in the city a variety that lends genuine interest. The description of the festival tells that the antebellum mansions are opened to the public, rich heirlooms displayed, and dames and damsels in hoop skirts and bobbing curls give gracious greetings to the guests during the celebration.

This sounds so much like our Santa Fe Fiesta ought to be, I thought. Our mansions have crumbled back to the earth from which they sprung. Nevertheless, if we were to ransack our mothers' old trunks, I believe we would find some fine old-fashioned silk gowns and jewels. So far we have been seeing mostly what Americans have arranged.

In those years, I had become accustomed to only a few hours of sleep. During the hours I lay awake that night I planned a program for the coming fiesta, just two months ahead. The following morning, full of enthusiasm, I called five ladies who I thought would be interested in helping to carry out my plans. Inviting them to tea, I told them I had something interesting to propose. This must have aroused their curiosity, as the five ladies came. I told them my plan, which was to try to arouse more interest amongst our Spanish-speaking population in taking part in the fiesta in greater numbers and that each of us six invite ten more to join us in the procession to the church, wearing old-fashioned gowns, in the procession to the cross, wearing shawls, that we should enter the parade on horseback as *"Las Galleras de Santa Ana,"* and to serve a Spanish barbecued supper. While it sounded like a large undertaking, nevertheless the ladies liked it. I exceeded my quota and invited about twenty from the elite of the Spanish families of the city. From four meetings, which I held, I had the program fairly well started. I also had planned to have during the last day of the fiesta a street dance. I went around trying to organize a society of *"Los Caballeros,"* and invited about thirty men. They all said "Yes," very nicely, when I talked to them, but only three couples came to the dance practices at the armory, so I gave up that idea.

The Fiesta Council, having heard about my activities, elected me to be a member and sent me an invitation to attend the weekly meetings. A week before the fiesta, the

174

council asked that my group elect the Fiesta Queen. In great haste, I called a meeting of my charter members with two others. After much discussion, we elected Miss Espinosa as Fiesta Queen and notified the council of our choice. For political reasons, I imagine, which I never dreamed would enter into the matter, the council replied that we would have to choose another. I explained that this would be very embarrassing to the young lady, as she had already ordered her costume and notified her relatives. She was then accepted.

Other worries, too, had to come to me. A few days before the fiesta, Miss Ortiz, whom I had named to assist me with the barbecued dinner, called me, saying she was leaving town with her mother, who was ill. I had already made all of the arrangements for the use of the vacant lot by the Elk's Club and for the kitchen. Now, I called another meeting and changed the barbecue into a Spanish chocolate *Merienda*. Among the ten members who came we furnished the refreshments, and I obtained the use of the patio and the kitchen at the Art Museum. After calling some half dozen people, I was finally granted permission to bring the piano out to the patio so Mrs. Hernandez might sing some Spanish songs during the serving of the *merienda*. We all wore old-fashioned gowns or silk shawls while serving.

Now, I turned my attention to obtaining horses for those members who were to ride in the parade. Horses were scarce, but at Agua Fria village I found three and at the United States cavalry stables, four. Some of the ladies feared that the horses might get frightened by all the noise and only five of us entered the parade. I had the words, *"Galleras de Santa Ana,"* written in large black letters on the white sheets covering the horses. This and the old-fashioned costumes worn by the riders brought forth so much applause that we won one of the prizes.

In spite of all the difficulties and disappointments, my program had worked out fairly well; so, at the meeting held after the fiesta I reported that our expenses had amounted to only six dollars for renting of the horses and the moving of the piano and table out to the patio. They were all so pleased, we decided to organize as a permanent society. Recalling that J. Frank Dobie, president of the Texas Folklore Society, had invited me to join his society, it occurred to me that as we did not have one here in New Mexico, it would be an excellent plan to start one. We named it *"La Sociedad Folklorica,"* although I was not sure that I had the correct word. *"La Folklorica"* is still the name of it today; and first rules which I drafted still govern the organization. These rules were that the society should be composed of only thirty members, all of whom must be of Spanish descent, and that the meetings must be conducted in the Spanish language, with the aim of preserving our language, customs and traditions.

By the second year of the fiesta celebration, I had conceived the idea of having an old-fashioned style show in connection with the Spanish tea. At Mrs. Warren's suggestion, I made arrangements to hold it in the patio at *Sena Plaza,* where we have held it for more than ten years, as that location furnishes the proper setting.

Several years before, my sister-in-law had brought my daughter a lovely silk gown which had belonged to her mother. It was all ripped apart and I had to be guided by old-fashioned pictures when sewing it together. The silk was so gorgeous, it was about the showiest gown modeled at our old-fashioned show.

For the members who did not have old-fashioned gowns, I searched the city and even wrote to relatives and friends in other towns. Many gowns which our ancestors had brought over the old trails and which were free from damage by moths and splits, were found, all ready to leap out of old trunks from the past to the present and have their wrinkles shaken out in the air, to portray the styles of by-gone days.

By the date for the annual fiesta, we had about twenty pretty gowns to be shown at our tea, and some fine silk embroidered shawls.

In the Monday historical parade we entered two floats, one in charge of Miss Sena, on which she displayed old-fashioned furniture. On the seats sat four of our members as *"Las Comadres."* The other float was in charge of clever Miss Espinosa. On this, there stood three brides, attired in beautiful old-style wedding gowns, their little train bearers wearing hooped skirts and long curls. On the floor sat an Indian maid drawing long strings of pearls and gold chains out of a large jewel box, *"las donas"* the gift brought to the bride by the bridegroom.

From this small beginning our style show and *merienda* have grown to be an important event each year at the fiesta. We now model about thirty very beautiful old-fashioned silk and velvet gowns. Embroidered silk shawls imported by way of Mexico from China and Spain, lace *mantillas,* fine pearl and gold jewelry, precious heirlooms all handed down from past generations, delight the eyes of more than three hundred people, to whom we serve our spicy chocolate and dainty Spanish pastries.

During the second year after I had organized the *Folklorica,* Miss Knott, the director of National Folk Festivals, wrote, advising me that she would stop here on her way to the festival at Dallas, and wished to meet me. I at once arranged a small folklore program in her honor, to be given the evening of her arrival at La Fonda Hotel. She was so pleased that she extended us an invitation to attend the Dallas Folk Festival.

Miss Hazel Hyde was kind enough to lend me her lovely patio for a Spanish card party and, later, her studio for a dance. We gave other programs for the purpose of raising funds that we might take a group of our folk dancers and singers, but failed to raise enough to cover the expenses of the trip.

CHAPTER XXIX

The Coronado Centennial

In 1940, during the celebration of the Coronado Cuarto Centennial, our society sponsored, at our own expense, some of the Spanish dramas. For *"Los Moros,"* the first drama given by the Oñate expedition in New Spain. we obtained costumes for the players. The shepherds' play called *"Los Pastores"* was the only drama which had been costumed before.

A gorgeous pageant was also sponsored by the Centennial Commission. This was held at Major's Park. Through the green hills sheltering our city was again heard the tramp of the mighty conquerors and from out of the shadows of the bygone centuries appeared the glittering armored, richly-appareled Spanish knights. Riding their richly-caparisoned steeds, they thundered down the hills, followed by *carretas* crowded with women and children, servants and gray-hooded monks. In the shelter of the hills, they camped. The smoke from the campfires arose to heaven, like incense, mingled with the murmur of thanksgiving prayers. The music of the string guitars and the joyful songs brought with them from Old Spain were suddenly hushed by the Indian war cries echoing through the hills. Closer and closer came the rhythm of the *tombe* beat, and the soft tread of moccasined feet. Women and children ran, seeking shelter. Men seized spears and swords and jumped on their steeds, prepared to

178

THE CORONADO CENTENNIAL

repulse the attack. It was a spectacular act viewed and heard through a public address by thousands of people.

For the closing of this Cuarto Centennial celebration to be held in El Paso, I was honored by being elected chairman of this section by the state chairman, Mr. Dicken, to assist in the closing program. I had to work rapidly so that my group of twenty folk dancers, musicians and singers might be rehearsed and prepared to make the trip to El Paso. Among them was a couple eighty years old who wished to attend so much that I procured passes for them. They danced with so much zest and grace that the newspapers not only gave them a nice "write-up," but also took their pictures. My group had such a wonderful time both sightseeing in El Paso and visiting in Juarez. We were lodged in a nice hotel, and it was an event which they still remember with pleasure.

June 15 was the tenth anniversary of the founding of the *Folklórica Sociedad*. It was celebrated in a whole day's round of social affairs, starting in the morning with high mass at the cathedral and the blessing of the new statue of St. Ann, the patroness chosen by the society. The members of the society attended the services in full, old-style costumes. From there they proceeded to the banquet held at La Fonda Hotel. Our eminent Archbishop Byrne and the three prelates who officiated at the church ceremonies honored us with their presence. The archbishop in his talk encouraged our work of preserving our Spanish traditions and the study of the Spanish language. His secretary, wishing to break away from the serious address of his eminence, introduced the witty anecdote about a teacher who, having given his pupils a talk about keeping up their traditions, after school noticed one of his boys sitting upon a fence very intent in his work. "What are you doing?" asked the teacher. "Sewing buttons on my pants to keep up my traditions," answered the boy.

As the organizer of the society, many honors were showered on me. A committee of past presidents escorted me to the church. At the banquet I was presented with an ex-

179

pensive silver gift. Flowers were sent to me by other friends. At the grand ball which closed the celebration I was asked to lead the grand march.

That winter at a meeting held at *Quinta Rosita,* the beautiful residence of one of our members we had a distinguished guest, Professor Mendoza from the University of Mexico. He was also president of the *Folklórica Sociedad* there. The meeting turned to a social one. By singing snatches of songs with piano accompaniment, the professor gave us demonstrations of how he traced a song from the place of its origin through the various changes which it had undergone in different countries. A reception was held in his honor at the close of the program. For this meeting, each member had been requested to bring a guest. The following morning Dr. and Mrs. Mendoza called to see me, and were very much interested in obtaining copies of my three books. A few weeks later, I received a very nice letter from them, telling me that my books constituted a great contribution to folklore. They sent two volumes of their society's folklore collections. The contributions, made mostly by member professors, are most valuable.

CHAPTER XXX

Again La Villa Celebrates

During the war the Santa Fe Fiesta was shortened to a two-day celebration, embracing only the principal historical events to maintain the tradition. Nevertheless, it was colorful. The crowning of the Fiesta queen was held at Major's Park. Joy and sadness mingled at this celebration. When the mayor in his address called the attention of the audience to the huge bonfire burning on the summit of Sun Mount in memory of our heroes who had lost their lives during the war, one could hear the sobs of relatives and friends throughout the assembly.

The 1946 fiesta also was short, but was attended by a larger, gayer crowd. On Sunday morning the procession which escorted the archbishop and the visiting prelates, led by the Fiesta Queen and her court and all past queens and princesses, was lovely. The singing by the seminary choir was very beautiful, and the eloquent sermon preached by Bishop Fitzsimmons of Amarillo was most impressive. Recounting the historical incident of the reconquest of New Mexico by Gen. de Vargas, he mentioned the coincidence that this year we were also commemorating the centennial of the conquest by Gen. Kearney, and he mentioned the freedom and great progress which had come to our state through these two conquests. He said that New Mexico was on the

181

verge of a new era with the discovery of the atomic bomb here on our soil.

While we pause to estimate with gratefulness the benefits we have derived since our sunny state took its place in the American union, let us pray that this new era may be one of as great benefit to us, and that the question of peace, which is still undetermined, may soon be settled in justice to all.

As our *Folklórica Sociedad* has become better known, it has become more and more popular, and we have been invited to sponsor many social functions, the last being a Spanish tea for the entertainment of about fifty members of the Music Federation while they were here for a three-day conference.

This was one of the most gracious and appreciative groups of ladies I have ever met. Music and art enrich the spirit and have a refining effect on the character of a person. It is high artistic culture that makes life interesting.

For two hours we enjoyed their company in the open patio of the old Palace of the Governors, where we served the refreshments. They were charmed with our old-fashioned gowns and lace mantillas, especially the one I was wearing, which had belonged to my mother and which has a floral design embroidered in colors. A very young lady with the group who had several times asked me to pause for pictures with groups which had come from various cities, embracing me, said: "You don't mind my loving you. You are so nice. You remind me of our French people in France." What happy memory had I brought to her mind? While our Spanish *tipica* orchestra played, we gave for them an exhibition of a few Spanish folk dances. A few weeks later I received a very nice letter from the state president, Mrs. Kastning, telling me how much they had enjoyed the party and, also, in reading my book, which I had autographed for her, and that she hoped to learn some Spanish from it.

Our *Folklórica Sociedad* has added more activities each year. At Easter we have the *Cascarones* Ball, when each member contributes three dozen egg shells that have been decorated and filled with perfumed confetti. The guests have great fun breaking these on the heads of their dance partners, much to their surprise and amusement.

On July 26, the federation celebrated the feast of St. Ann. The medical sisters also have St. Ann as their patroness, and invited us to hold the celebration at their house. In a candle-light procession the statue of St. Ann was brought from the home of the president of our society to the hospital. It was my turn to be hostess, and as I wished to perpetuate the tradition of the *velorios,* or wakes, I asked Sister Helen to come out to the gate with me, holding lighted candles, to meet the procession and burn incense before the statue. Then it was carried into the chapel where the chaplain priest, gave us the benediction. To further carry out the old customs, the singing of hymns was interspersed with prayers until ten o'clock, when refreshments were served instead of the midnight supper which the *mayordomo* of the wake used to serve.

To encourage greater interest in the preservation of the old Spanish customs and the study of our traditions, I donated to the society my fifty-page album with my folklore collection. The organizing of this *Folklórica Sociedad* has brought me a feeling of considerable satisfaction because it has awakened much interest among our Spanish population in learning and appreciating our old traditions.

The glamour and beauty which appeals to the senses of the artists and the writers who have come into our country, should appeal more forcefully to us, the heirs of the artistic culture and of the poetry and the religious traditions which our Spanish ancestors left to crystallize on the crests of our New Mexico mountains.

CHAPTER XXXI

Reunion of New Mexico Constitutional Convention Delegates

Judge Mabry, who had been the youngest member of the Constitutional Convention — that body which drafted the laws for the state of New Mexico prior to its admission into statehood — called a meeting of the surviving members.

Of the one hundred members of the 1912 convention, but twenty survived, and five of them were unable to attend because of ill health. The chief secretary, Mr. George Armijo, was also confined to the hospital. Two beautiful rose bouquets sent by Mrs. C. J. Roberts for the meeting in memory of her husband, one of the deceased members, were taken to Mr. Armijo at the hospital. The other clerk and two of the newspaper correspondents were present. Either the wife or the closest relative of each deceased member was invited to represent him at the meeting. As Judge Mabry called the name of each member, he rose and responded with a short speech. One of them recalled that in those days people took time to interpose wit along with the work to relieve the tedium and seriousness. He told this story:

When the invited priest started to intone the accustomed prayer at the opening of the Convention, Pedragon, the ever-ready interpreter, started to interpret the prayer in Spanish, only to be interrupted by Mr. Catron's loudly whispering, "Shut up, you fool; the Almighty understands English."

My husband, a delegate, told me another joke. The Republicans, who held a majority, were tired of the daily lambasting of the Chaves County Democratic delegate. They lured him into the home of one his friends, closed the door and quickly tacked a smallpox quarantine card on the door. Then they held him there until the convention had adjourned.

There were seven ex-governors present at this reunion, each of whom was asked to give a talk. Some of the wives also responded with speeches. Your author, not being a gifted speaker, only stood to acknowledge the generous applause with which the assembly greeted me when my name was called.

CHAPTER XXXII

Visiting at the Dear Village

On my last visit to Taos I found that the automobile has shrunk the distance from a two-day ride to a two-hour one. There is no trace left of the trails of Western beaver traders which led to this settlement, nor of the lively atmosphere imparted by visits of the gay mountain men, who came here to attend the plaza fairs. Instead of wagon teams and saddle ponies tied to the fence posts around the plaza park, one now sees a long line of parked cars. La Tule's gay gambling saloon at La Loma is now a quiet artist's studio. Taos has become the mecca of the artist. Three of the five outstanding artists in New Mexico make their homes there. In the magnificent mountain scenery and in the primitive Indian, the artist finds inspiration for his canvas; and in the unique mixture of customs, manner and dress, the writer finds material for his books. Although the population has more than doubled in the last decade, the town has retained its narrow streets and low, flat-roofed adobe houses. Some dub it as quaint, picturesque or strange. Some see only its customs rather than its soul, which is hidden to the unobservant stranger.

The attractive Don Fernando Hotel had been destroyed by fire, and a new La Fonda Hotel had opened for business. While I was waiting at the desk to see the clerk, a couple of

186

VISITING AT THE DEAR VILLAGE

tourists came in. The man, looking around the lobby, said, "This is the queerest place I have ever seen."

Always ready to speak up for my old towns, I said: "If you have seen Santa Fe, that is another interesting place. We keep our cities different."

My relatives and friends made my two days pleasant, inviting me to their homes. While having dinner at one of my nephew's homes, his wife told me how incensed they were with Fosster after reading his new book. "You ought to write an answer to it," she said.

After reading the book, I thought, yes, this book should be criticized. Fosster lacks sympathy and understanding about the poor underprivileged class who, on account of their poverty, lack a moral education and modern facilities for better living. He should have studied the customs of our country before attempting to write and not become confused about the Spanish, Mexican and Indian, wasting time and a God-given talent writing about the lower things in life.

After dinner, my nephew took me in his car for a visit to my old home at Arroyo Hondo. In fifteen minutes I found myself gliding down the once-steep hill, now almost level, and I was surprised to see before me the little sunken green valley. What a different aspect it now presented! High pitched roofs, a new, modern-looking schoolhouse — with nothing left but memories of our once lively, happy home, now in melting ruins. Only the foundation was left of the *capilla,* or chapel, of the Holy Family which my father had so devotedly cared for and repaired as long as his health permitted him to go there. With a sigh, I turned away from this sad sight. Some months ago I read an article written by the Reverend Crocchiola in the *Register* about his visit to what he calls the "quaint little village," which held more fascination for him than any other village in New Mexico. "It's a beauty spot," he goes on to say, "visited by only a few, because but few know of its culture, its antiquity and its history." He describes as the most interesting item in the old church (which, in confusion, he calls the famous *capilla*), the carved wooden statue of Our Lady of Sorrows. On Good

187

Fridays, when the little statue was placed on a little table in the middle of the church during the prayer of the stations of the cross, mother called it *"Nuestra Señora de la Soledad,"* "Our Lady of Solitude." The lady seemed to have a sadder and a lonelier expression that day. My Aunt Soledad dressed the statue in a black silk taffeta dress, which stood out in full folds, like her own. Miguel de Herrera, the Santero, had used my aunt as his model. He did better at his primitive art than in playing the fiddle at mass.

It was my good fortune while I was on this visit, staying at the home of one of my brothers, that the priest came from Taos to celebrate a special mass in honor of Our Lady of the Rosary. My nephew took his mother and me to the church. I was so thrilled to see the old upper village, which I had not seen since my marriage. The village had not changed, but in remodeling the church the huge buttresses which supported the front wall had been removed and the building had lost its interesting aspect of old mission churches. The interior had also been renovated; even the little statue of Our Lady of The Rosary had received a white and pink "retoque" on her dainty face, and dressed in a new shimmering white satin gown, veil and flower wreath. She was taken from the lace covered table in a procession around the church, as in my younger days while we sang and prayed.

My brother had renovated the store, so that it seemed a new building, thus erasing the last proof of its attractive old front. Such a lack of appreciation and interest in preserving what might now have been a most attractive guest house or inn, as what is left of the building is on the highway. Crowded buses on their way to Colorado, roar by twice a day. The automobile has curtailed distances, and swiftly replaced isolation with association by contact with centers of modern activity, and has brought a modern trend even to remote areas. The stores in the village now furnish the homes with baker's bread and pastries and all kinds of canned goods, so that the housekeepers do not have to spend as much time in the kitchen. They now find time to go to town, to attend a movie, to do their shopping and to buy clothing for their

VISITING AT THE DEAR VILLAGE

families, ready-made. Yet I heard some of them complain that it is such hard work to live in the country. They fail to appreciate the comforts they are enjoying. Only two of my brothers have remained on the lands which my father gave them, and they are doing well, have nice homes and have reared nice families of well-educated children.

Country work must serve as a long-life stimulant, for my mother, although possessing a delicate constitution, lived past her seventieth year, and my father was past ninety-one when he died. They both had a peaceful ending. They had no remorse; they had lived in peaceful goodwill towards everyone, and they had done their duty and had done it well, always satisfied, detached from petty worries, a useful preservative measure.

The time came to end my visit, to leave the sunny, sheltered little valley which imparts a sense of security. Within a few days one recaptures a serenity of spirit and a restfulness in the peaceful silence which surrounds it. It would be a sweet ending to live there the rest of my days; but duties called me back to the dust and noise of our city, which, thirty years of modern progress has changed from a small, quiet town to a city with over thirty thousand in population, full of the noise of the speedy striving of competition. Nevertheless, we are still striving to preserve some of its unique attractiveness by retaining the old New Mexico style of architecture, and the historical and traditional religious celebrations, which each year attracts more newcomers to our "city different," as it is now called. Our elegant, new La Fonda Hotel has taken the place of the old La Fonda Inn located at the end of the famous Santa Fe Trail. The historic three-foot thick walls of the old Palace, seat of executive power for centuries under three governments, still stand as sturdy and solid as three hundred years ago when they were built.

As one grows older, the clock turns faster. Another year has rolled by, scarcely observed, and we again found ourselves celebrating.

The 1947 Santa Fe Fiesta was lengthened to a four-day

189

celebration. It also increased in the number of celebrants. Some two thousand cars honked their way to Fort Marcy to witness the burning of *Zozobra*. To accommodate the large attendance dance at the *merienda* of our *Folklorica Sociedad,* we had to hold the style show twice and serve refreshments to different groups. It merely takes someone who will trouble to stir up interest, to learn what people can do. Our members had rehabilitated that year more than thirty lovely old gowns, which during the first years were so difficult to obtain. These are the remaining proof of that richer era when our ancestors reigned supreme in this land, when the dress, manners and customs of Old Spain were echoed here in New Spain. Music as it was in days of old at every social gathering lends greatly to our *merienda* program. The fiesta queen and her court presided. Our eminent Archbishop Byrnes crowned the fiesta queen on a platform so built that the fully-illuminated open door of the cathedral formed a beautiful backdrop. While Miss Fernandez sang "La Paloma," three doves were let out of a cage to take their flight over the heads of the group on the platform and of the spectators. In the sermon which the visiting Archbishop of Peoria delivered at the fiesta mass, he stressed the great need of spiritual solidarity among nations, to give them strength to bear the burden of the unavoidable friction which in these restless times is taking place in the world. Right here in this land which for centuries has cradled, and bears so deeply, the imprints of the great religion of the world, its peace is now disturbed by the proximity of the atomic hatchery holding us for better or for destruction.

CHAPTER XXXIII

Rhythm in Adobe

Since living in this ancient city I have become so attached to antiques that I tenaciously refuse to part with my old, five-room adobe. It is part of the former twenty-room mansion of the once wealthy Don Clemente Ortiz. My father bought the property from Don Clemente and had it remodeled into three apartments for renting. My father gave one of my brothers the north wing, and when I found that living alone in my bungalow was too lonely for me, I thought of moving closer to my parents and bought the south wing, a five-room apartment. I then had the inside renovated to make it more comfortable, but left the outside unchanged, except for planting grass, flowers and vines along the front porch, which, fortunately, had been left in the old style. It took a great deal of work to clean out the piles of rubbish in the backyard, left by tenants and accumulating for years, and to remove half-burnt woodsheds and other unsightly things. Within two years I had a nice garden there, with climbing red roses peeping into my dining room window, and Heavenly Blue morning glories twining over the panes in my sun room. A three-room apartment which I built, encloses the garden and furnishes an attractive, secluded back patio. Here on a seat under the lilac bush my Angie and I would sit on cool summer evenings, she singing to the accompaniment of her ukulele, while I sewed or just rested, listening to her songs. I recall those pleasant evenings when now I sit there alone, absorbed in my work of writing or reading to keep from becoming too lonely and discouraged.

For more than ten years people have been coming, trying to buy my house. "I like the location," they tell me. And when they see the nearly three-foot thick inside walls, they add, "And these substantial walls." I like them, too. I have become so attached to their warmth, and the deep window sills which furnish me space on which to keep my only living companions, my flowering plants. This house is a symbol of the past which I love — from the birds' nests on the *vigas* of my front porch to the birds' decorations trickling down my whitewashed walls. They remind me of the black swallows' nests which covered the *vigas* on the porch of our *capilla*. The nests became so infested with fleas that mother had them torn down, and I lost one of my amusements: I had loved to watch the industrious birds flying back and forth, incessantly carrying bits of mud and pasting them in layers round and round their beehive-shaped nests until only a little round hole was left as an opening, through which the birds woud squeeze and turn around and peep at me. I do not know why this species was called the *"cimarronas,"* or wild swallows, for they look the same as the domestic species, except that the domestic species build their nests like a pocket, round at the bottom and straight across at the open top. They were friendly birds, and built their nests on the same *vigas,* chattering all the time as if they very happy at being undisturbed at their work.

Here in my patio I also have noticed how nervous the red-breasted songbirds are. They pause on the telephone line, twitching their little heads, awaiting a quiet moment to fly to their nests. In their haste they drop half the feathers and straw they are carrying to build their nests. Their songs are so interrupted by noises that they hardly ever give them the finishing note. I have heard these birds really give out with songs in the country, where they carried on a regular contest, answering each other. From the swallow we hear no song; why this ugly black bird has been chosen as a theme

RHYTHM IN ADOBE

for so many lovely and romantic Spanish songs I don't know.

Gradually I had detached myself from the country home. In memory I still keep alive and cherish the thirty years or more of peaceful and happy living there. Time has brought changes there, too. Every bush and tree which I planted has grown so tall, obstructing the beautiful view of the green fields and mountains which we used to see from the front porch. Clouds of dust raised by speeding cars traveling along the graveled highway in front of the house, also obscure the view. The Spanish-American Normal School, which my husband founded, has grown into a big institution. Several large buildings now fill the beautifully landscaped grounds. How well repaid my husband would feel for the struggle which he made to obtain this school, if he coud revisit it and observe the progress made there. He always seemed to see far ahead. When the legislature finally appropriated the money for the first building he said to me, "This is going to be a very good thing for these poor country boys who cannot afford to go to expensive schools." About three hundred boys and girls receive their education there annually. My husband rests from his labors, but his work carries on.

Since I sold my county home three years ago, I have not been there again. It is not easy to become reconciled to seeing someone else occupying the nook which one has cherished. Moreover, juvenile delinquency has reached even the country village. Each summer that I went there it cost me so much in wasted strength and money, repairing broken windows and other things which were destroyed just for the fun of doing mischief; so I had to part with the house.

In appreciation, I must mention how my good friends, members of my *Folklorica* society, most agreeably surprised me on the fifteenth anniversary of my founding the society. The members very-quietly gathered at my front door with a couple of musicians, and gave me a gay serenade. When I opened the door each one greeted me with a warm embrace as they came in and then addressed with me an affectionate verse that each one had composed to me. One of them presented me with a bouquet of beautiful roses. They all looked charming in their pretty costumes and with red roses in their hair. The rest sang and danced in the best spirits while two of the members quietly slipped out and brought in the refreshments. When we were invited to come into the dining room, they had the table decorated with roses, and there was a beautiful frosted cake with my name and a good wish written on it. I was asked to cut the first slice. I felt as if I were again at my wedding, and I was overcome by this expression of my *Folklorica's* friendship and great esteem that although feeling very happy, I could not keep back my tears. They have made me recipient of so many honors. At the last Santa Fe Fiesta, they again honored me with a lovely gesture, by having the two velvet-clad pages of the fiesta queen escort me to sit with the queen and her court on her throne. This 1954 Fiesta found me greeting the famous Cardinal Spellman from New York City, at the reception given in his honor at the archbishop's garden.

I will always treasure these incidents as the happiest and most cherished in these latter years of my life.

As a member of the Santa Fe Women's Club and Library Association since its organization more than forty years ago, I have had the opportunity of meeting many interesting personalities from all over the United States. Some of them have been invited to speak; others have given pleasure with their music and song. It is not only the enjoyment from seeing our friends or from getting acquainted with new ones that are rewarding, but how much one may learn if an interest in the various club activities is developed.

At one monthly meeting, Dr. Friedman delivered a very enlightening talk about the past years' extensive research that has been carried on in a hunt for the cure of cancer. The last article I read told about experiments in using atomic energy as a cure.

In a recent April during the convention of the State

Federation of Women's Clubs, it was our pleasure to entertain some one hundred members representing the clubs of different cities in the state. Mrs. Dickinson, the General Federation president, flew from Washington, D. C., to attend the convention and to honor us with her presence. During this meeting, there were held two outstanding social events — one, a banquet sponsored by the State Federation and supervised by the members of the Santa Fe Club, was held at La Fonda; the other was the reception and tea held at the Governor's Mansion.

Some weeks after the convention, I received a letter from Mrs. Dickinson graciously telling me that she had read my book on the airplane on her return to Washington and had enjoyed it very much.

When kind Archbishop Gerkin told Mrs. Hull that a cathedral parish female charity organization ought to be organized, she invited ten ladies who elected me chairman. I told her my ambition for years had been to have a free clinic for our poor people, and that I had written to some wealthy Denver ladies for donations to start one but never received an answer. We went and told the Bishop and he donated the clinic building we have now.

The work in the Charity Committee has brought me closer to our native population and made me better acquainted with their great needs. A poverty greater than the one I found in the native villages in which I lived, I found here. There everyone owned his two or three little rooms and kept them neatly repaired. Here I find large families living crowded in one or two little rooms with leaking roofs and wanting every repair. Why did you leave your country home and farm? I ask them. To bring the children to school, is their excuse, but the cost of paying rent and buying commodities, living out of the store, and the men taking to drink, cause the poor families always to be in need of help. I find them very grateful for any help given them. Their thanks come in these words, "Dios se lo pague." ("God repay you.") They show their gratitude by the friendly greetings I receive on every side, by old and young. This is a great compensation for the privilege of being able to help.

I miss these attentions when I am in a town out of our state. I get homesick and return to work, although doctors advise, "Rest and relax; go to a movie." I do when there is something worth seeing. In the movie, "Young Abe Lincoln," I saw such great resemblance between Abe and Ven after my husband's face became lined. His eyes were deep-set, he had the same shaped forehead, slight humped nose, dimpled chin and even the same mannerism. Lincoln sitting with his chair tipped back, feet on top of his desk, thumbs thrust in the armholes of his vest, lips puffed when in deep thought — this was a perfect picture of how I sometimes saw Ven in his office.

"Don't you get lonesome living alone?" people ask me. With so many hobbies to fill my time, what time have I to become lonesome? Just now, when I am about to close my narrative, my cousin, Mercedes Lucero, has sent me an article about our family which her mother had asked her to write for Miss Mary Wheelwright. When this lady bought Uncle Luis' home at *Los Luceros,* she wished to know the family history. A few years later when Miss Wheelwright was traveling in Europe, Aunt Marina received a letter from her, saying, "Here in a little corner in Spain I have found the village of *Los Luceros* — your ancestors."

At one of the meetings last winter of our *Folklórica Sociedad,* Dr. Reginald Fisher of the American School of Research spoke to us. He asked the members if we would write and give him the genealogy of our families for a book, which he is compiling on the history of the early Spanish families in the state. From Aunt Marina's notes, I was able to add three more pages to the fifteen which I had already taken to Dr. Fisher.

At the meeting of the Archaeological Society a few weeks ago, I greatly enjoyed the address by the brilliant Dr. Von Kleinschmidt, chancellor of the University of California. He was invited to speak at the memorial services and the unveiling of the bust and plaque of bronze, a gift to the museum by the Archaeological Society in memory of the late Dr. Hewett, as president of the society for so many years. Dr. Hewett accomplished an admirable amount of work in the field of archaeology in this state and in Central America.

Who knows? One historian says that the first white men who discovered the Ojo Caliente Mineral Springs were soldiers from Sosa's contigent. Others say they were Cabeza de Vaca's soldiers. For my part I like to believe in the legend written about Ponce de Leon and say:

Here I find myself, like Ponce de Leon, seeking the "Fountain of Youth." When Cabeza de Vaca's soldiers were coming up the *Rio del Norte,* they branched off and followed a smaller river to the northeast. They came into a narrow valley and saw steam rising from a crevice in the hills. As they were curious to learn what it might be, they crossed the river and found hot water oozing out of the earth. These Spaniards wrote back to Spain that they had discovered in the hills some springs of hot water so rich in minerals that the Indians who lived above it thought their gods had sent them these waters to cure their ills. They further wrote, "We are naming this place *'Ojo Caliente.'* " Later came Ponce de Leon seeking these wonderful springs. When he found them, he called them the "Fountain of Youth." He named them correctly.

For more than forty years I have visited these springs, and I have seen and heard of numerous remarkable cures. These marvelous waters do not take the years away from us but, with restored health, the spirit and mind are renewed into a new fountain of energy.

People are yet kindly remarking on my imposing stature. I said to the attendant who had neglected to look in my bathroom door, "You are not worrying about my drowning in that big tub of water?" She laughingly replied, "I shall look in the next time to see if you have gone down the drain pipe." This was an embarrassing remark to make to me before the half dozen one hundred and sixty pounders,

197

who were there trying to get rid of some of their excessive avoirdupois through evaporation. These remarks about my size will not cease until people see me in my casket. Then the remarks will change from, "She is just like a doll," to "What a little old lady!"

The first time I visited these springs they were owned by Mr. Antonio Joseph, who was at one time our delegate to Congress. The first building was a small frame hotel, propped up on cobblestone supports, so the river water could run underneath without washing it away in floods. This frame structure has been replaced by two nice hotel buildings and several apartments and cabins. Bus lines bring guests from every state in the Union. Modern progress has made of these springs a fountain of wealth as well as of health. Mrs. Joseph was a smart woman and must have had a vision of what this place would some day be. When her only son, Antonio, was anxious to sell and move to the city with his beautiful wife, Angela, his mother strongly objected. Nevertheless, he sold out. Several years later I visited Mrs. Joseph in Denver. The lady was badly crippled and living in a small apartment with her two granddaughters. They had lost all they had of this world's goods. Angela had been killed in her own airplane while competing in an air race, and poor Antonio had about lost his mind. "I don't like it here. I wish I were at Ojo," Mrs. Joseph said to me. How perishable is the wealth of the world; only good deeds endure.

Each time I come to the end of my story, something happens to incite me to continue writing a little longer. Now, it is the Reverend Keller's address over the B. C. Hour of Faith, urging us to join in the fight against immoral books and plays by replacing them with good ones. Mr. Hoover also says in one of his addresses, "Every follower of Christ should unite in bringing men's thoughts into a better trend of mind for the decent, moral things in life." This sounds to me like a challenge for everyone who can to make an effort to help, no matter how poor our talents may be. Yes,

RHYTHM IN ADOBE

I must contribute my bit. I must try to put this little work on the market and, also, the two plays which I have "snitched" from my first book. For now at this book's close, I am also coming to close the seventy-fifth year of my life. Fifty years ago I would have thought it incredible that such a little frail being as I, should have been blest with the gift of all these years.

Once at my piano lesson, Sister Rosana held my little finger over the note and pulled my thumb, trying to help me reach an octave; and, with all the stretching, my hand could barely reach it. With a sigh, she said to me, "Cleofas, promise that you will not get married before you are twenty-five." "Yes, Sister," I answered. There was no need to promise; I had placed the span of my life to be fifteen years. I don't know why I was so conscious of my physical frailty, except that people were always remarking about my tiny size. After I passed the fifteen year mark, I moved it up to eighteen. At this time, cupid came, as we say in Spanish, *"en su caballo ligero"* ("riding his fast horse"), and made me forget the promise and all else; I set sail on the matrimonial bark without thought or worry. My Romeo liked me as I was. What more would I wish?

I find that the many blessings which have been showered upon me during my long life outweigh all the ills and troubles, and that I have much for which to be thankful — for the interesting work which has filled my varied life, drowning all care; for the sincere friends which I have retained throughout my life, (I have never lost a friend except those that death has parted from me — all of whom I have greatly missed); for the happiness of my early life sheltered from all care by good parents; for good brothers and sister; for a loving husband and a dear daughter who cheered and encouraged me in my saddest moments; and, above all, for the gift of faith when later in life things changed for me. For all of this and much more, let my most grateful thanksgiving ascend to the throne of the Almighty God who orders all things well.

199

ROMANCE OF A LITTLE VILLAGE GIRL

For all through the darkness
Of mist or of wrong,
I have found solace in prayer,
In faith and in love.

THE END